LIVE THE DREAM

No More Excuses

LIVE THE DREAM

NO MORE EXCUSES

Larry Winters

CENTER STREET

New York • Boston • Nashville

BSM 56900

Center Street
Hachette Book Group
237 Park Avenue
New York, NY 10017

www.centerstreet.com

Printed in the United States of America
RRD-C

First Edition: April 2012

10 9 8 7 6 5 4 3 2

Center Street is a division of Hachette Book Group, Inc.
The Center Street name and logo are trademarks of Hachette Book Group, Inc.

The Hachette Speakers Bureau provides a wide range of authors for speaking events. To find out more, go to www.hachettespeakersbureau.com or call (866) 376-6591.

The publisher is not responsible for websites (or their content) that are not owned by the publisher.

Library of Congress Cataloging-in-Publication Data

Winters, Larry.
    Live the dream : no more excuses / Larry Winters.—1st ed.
        p. cm.
    ISBN 978-1-4555-1362-8
    1. Winters, Larry. 2. Success in business. 3. Entrepreneurship. 4. Success.
5. Businessmen—United States. I. Title.
    HF5386.W594 2012
    658.4'09—dc23   2011047625

I dedicate this book to my awesome wife, Pam. Without a doubt, she has been EVERYTHING I have needed to get to this point in my life. She has been with me since the very beginning and has been a rock for me when I did dumb things and made huge mistakes. I unintentionally put her in situations that most women would have never tolerated, and not only did she stay, but she loved me through them.

Thank you, Pam. You've been a great mom to our three children, a perfect match for me with my "special" personality, and a superb business partner. It has been a wonderful journey.

And to my mom and dad, Helen and George Winters. Both taught me the value of hard work. More specifically, working hard for yourself. When I was growing up, Dad owned and operated an Atlantic Richfield service station. He always told me it was much better to work for your own dreams and goals rather than someone else's. I saw my mom work at any job she could just to support my dad's start-up income at the gas station. They both showed me what it meant to do whatever it takes to make your business successful.

I'm so blessed and grateful to have such a great wife and parents.

You are the best! I love you.

Contents

*Statements flagged with an asterisk (*) are subject
to the policy available in the Appendix.*

ACKNOWLEDGMENTS

Writing a book was never in my wildest dreams. But when the idea was presented, I started thinking about all the people who helped me, mentored me, encouraged me, and, yes, pushed me to be the very best I could possibly be, and I realized that sharing the lessons I learned on how to build a successful and fulfilling business was a great opportunity to encourage others just getting started or struggling through tough times.

When I stopped making excuses, committed myself to settling for nothing but success, and invested my time with other hardworking, like-minded people, I started to live the dream and haven't looked back since! So many people need to be thanked for the contributions they made to help me realize my dreams.

Special thanks to Mike Bundy, the first to join my team, and his wife, Susan. Your friendship, patience, tenacity, and, most of all, your confidence that we could succeed have helped Pam and me beyond any words I can express.

Thanks to the best leadership team I've ever worked with, including: Gary and Nancy Ayers, Toby and Mia Ayers, Jake and Jackie Baker, Greg and Jacquie Francis, Matt and Alana Grotewold, Campbell and Dianne Haigh, Roger and Roxanne Holt, Alan and Michele Leininger, Joe and Marybeth Markiewicz, Gary and Tammy Newell, Danny and Renate

Snipes, Terry and Lorri Taylor, Doug and Amie Weir, and Mike and Jana Waechter. Each of you continues to challenge me every day to keep growing and learning.

Thanks to Zig Ziglar, the "master motivator" and author of *See You at the Top* and dozens of other books, who continues to inspire me. And to Og Mandino, author of *The Greatest Salesman in the World* and other great books, who taught me the fundamentals of selling that I still practice today.

Thanks to Rich DeVos, Jody and Kathy Victor, Dexter and Birdie Yager, and all the leadership teams of Amway that helped me live the dream. I have written this book for entrepreneurs and small business owners. For nearly thirty years I have been blessed to be associated with the Amway Corporation, a great company with great people. I know the principles and practices I have learned and applied in my Amway business will help business men and women start and grow their own businesses, whatever type of product or service they are providing.

Thanks to John Maxwell, who helped me learn how to be a servant leader, and to Kenneth and Gloria Copeland, who helped me draw nearer and nearer to my Lord and Savior, Jesus Christ.

Thanks to Nancy Alcorn and Coach K, who are two great examples of dedication and leadership strength in tough times.

Thanks to all those unnamed but faithful friends, associates, and independent business owners. Thank you for being my inspiration to live the dream every day! I hope this book transforms your thinking in a whole new realm of living and working.

And finally, thanks to Rush McComas, my best high school friend who passed away too soon, but to whom I will forever be indebted for the fun we shared in the business and the joy he always brought to my heart.

LIVE THE DREAM

No More Excuses

1

Drowning in a Car Wash

Who has never tasted what is bitter does not know what is sweet.

—German proverb

There are some times in life you can never forget—even though you'd love to. For me, the year was 1985.

My wife, Pam, and I were happily married and raising a young family, yet I felt as though I was a complete failure as a provider. Nothing seemed to be working, and the world was crashing in.

We were living in a nine-hundred-square-foot wood frame house that was built on a tiny lot just after World War II—and we were three months behind on the $225 rent. The pressure we were under was painful.

You should have seen the place. It was painted light green and had a driveway that held one and a half compact cars and had practically no backyard. The dirt-floor basement was unusable. To put it mildly, it was a mess.

When my checks bounced, the landlord would warn me, "Larry, this isn't working. You've got to get caught up. It can't go on like this!"

In truth, we were one sentence away from being homeless. There were many times when he could have said, "That's it. I am locking the doors and calling the sheriff."

If this had happened, we would have had to move in with either Pam's parents or mine. I shuddered at the very thought. What an embarrassment that would have been.

"Richer or Poorer"

While I was just getting started in my new business, I had tried selling cars to bring in some much-needed extra cash. But the car business was so bad in the mid-1980s that I decided to give it up and look for something else. Of course, the car dealership took back the Volkswagen Rabbit they had loaned me. Bingo! We had no transportation.

That January, my cousin and I decided to launch a lawn care business with a borrowed pickup truck. But the weather was too cold in North Carolina for the first couple of months, so we had very few customers. Finally, I started getting twenty or twenty-five dollars to mow a lawn or do odd jobs, but since we had to sink some cash into equipment, my bills were far outpacing my income.

Everything was financed—our furniture, even our television set. Before long I was as much as nine months behind on what I owed Visa, MasterCard, Household Finance, and bank loans. The pile of bills was growing higher and higher, and we owed everybody—including Pam's relatives.

I'd write checks for my phone and electric bills and pray I could somehow cover them before they bounced.

I had no credit, no car. I was buried in debt, barely keeping my head above water.

In April 1984, our daughter, Tara, was born. She was our pride and joy, and we scraped together what little we could to buy her baby food and diapers. We would visit our parents' home on the weekends—basically to get something to eat.

Pam and I often recited the vows that we made at our wedding: "For richer or poorer, for better or for worse."

Truer words were never spoken. We were certainly poorer—and things were progressively getting worse!

Shake, Rattle, and Roll!

Pam's parents were fully aware of the financial crisis we were going through, and they looked for ways to help. They told me, "We have this old car on our farm that isn't working. If we can get it up and running, you can use it."

What a sight it was! The 1977 Mustang II, a four-seat two door with over a hundred thousand miles on the speedometer, had been totaled twice and was sitting there with grass actually growing through the windows! It had no air-conditioning, and the seats were badly torn. I don't know how we managed, but we straightened out the frame and somehow got it repaired and licensed.

It was painted primer-gray, and there wasn't an ounce of gloss anywhere—just plenty of rust on the doors, the hood, and the fenders.

However, there was a much bigger problem. When I would reach fifty-five miles an hour, the car would begin to shimmy and shake so violently that I thought I'd lose control of the vehicle. It felt like the wheels were literally coming off! But, hey, at least it was transportation, so I just drove slower than I wanted to.

Our small rented house had a hundred-gallon kerosene heating tank. But at $1.50 a gallon, we could usually afford to feed it only about five gallons at a time. On cold nights, when the money ran out, so did the fuel.

This happened more than once. One evening when I arrived home, the water in the toilet was frozen solid and the dog's water bowl was frozen over, too.

I vividly remember the time our dog, unbeknownst to us, bumped into the kerosene heater in the middle of the night. The flame went out, but the furnace kept blowing. We woke up the next morning, and the entire room was dusted black. I looked at Pam, and she had black soot smudged under her eyes and black in her nostrils. She glanced over at me, and I asked, "Do I look as funny as you do?"

"Yes," she said, smiling.

The curtains were black; the walls were black. Then the dog jumped up on our bed—and even the spots around his eyes weren't white anymore!

In my mind's eye I can still see that modest house. One window had a broken pane for three years because we didn't have the money to repair it. Our furniture probably wouldn't have been welcome at a garage sale. It was nothing but junk.

I look back on those days and wonder how we ever survived. However, there was one possession I had that outweighed all the pressure, all the stress, and every negative. As unlikely as it may seem, down deep in my heart I had an overwhelming, all-consuming dream that could not be denied.

In this book I want to share the lessons I have learned

that I believe will get you to where you want to be whether you've experienced some success or you're newly struggling as I was. I am telling my story in this book because I have been out of work and in debt, and I understand all too well the feelings of despair and hopelessness.

I reached the point where I ran out of excuses, but I did have a choice. I decided to live my dream rather than remain in a rut.

Let me tell you what brought me to that point.

A Lesson from Dad

As a young teen growing up in west-central New Jersey, I remember a particular day when I was standing beside my dad while he was shaving. He paused for a moment, then looked at me in the reflection of the mirror and said, "Larry, you are smaller than most kids. But that just means you are going to have to try a little harder than the next guy. It doesn't mean you are any less of a person—you'll just have to work more."

His words were etched in my mind from that day forward. After all, I was about five feet five, so I knew I could never dunk a basketball, and I couldn't sing or dance—so there was no future in sports or as an entertainer.

My first exposure to self-employment was my father. He owned his own Atlantic Richfield gas station (now ARCO) at the corner of Baird Boulevard and Marlton Pike in Camden, New Jersey.

Growing up, I remember that practically everybody I knew and liked bought gas from my dad's station. Ours was a family business—and people supported us as if we were their relatives. If you needed a tune-up or a new set of tires, there was only one place for our friends to go: Dad's service station.

Unfortunately, today such loyalty has almost disappeared. Instead, people, feeling the economic crunch, look at the price of gas on the huge signs before deciding where to fill up.

In 1973, times were changing, and my dad sold his business (which had expanded into towing and auto salvage), and he announced, "We're moving to North Carolina." I was sixteen years old and wasn't exactly excited about leaving everything I knew and loved. But this wasn't my decision to make.

During my teen years, Dad was always telling me, "Son, you need to work for yourself and own your own business. It's the only way to go."

However, I couldn't relate to his advice. At school I was being told just the opposite: "Get a good education so you can find a good job." In other words, go to work for someone else, don't quit, and maybe you can retire when you're sixty-five.

Education wasn't exactly my thing. In school, the only subjects I excelled in were recess and gym. I hated math and science. To me, homeroom was the place to close my eyes and take a nap.

I spent practically all my spare time playing baseball, and I even convinced myself I had enough talent to make the pros. I told my folks, "I'm going to be a millionaire someday"—and I honestly believed I would make it to the major leagues.

After we settled into our new life in North Carolina, one summer I worked at the Bonanza Sirloin Pit as a busboy. At least it kept me busy and put a few dollars in my pocket. But there were Saturday afternoons when, during a break after lunch, I would stand on the back porch and look up at that clear Carolina blue sky dotted with white, puffy clouds.

Drinking in the fresh air, I would think, *If only I was waterskiing, out on the golf course, or riding dirt bikes with my buddies.*

Reluctantly, I'd go back inside and be all smiles, trying to do a good job, but it was almost more than I could take. *Why am I trapped in this restaurant?* I wondered. Here I was, scraping food off of dirty dishes when all I wanted to do was to be outdoors enjoying a beautiful day. But my day-dreaming was futile because I needed the money to pay for the used car I had bought.

Even at the age of sixteen, I longed to be free!

While in high school, to make a few extra bucks, I began working at the Constan Car Wash for $2.30 an hour. It was a brick structure on Old Wake Forest Road in Raleigh, North Carolina, that had a hundred-foot pull-through tunnel, five full-service bays, and a cashier's booth.

You should have seen me in those high school days. I wore long hair down to my shoulders and was trying to grow a mustache—but my upper lip looked like a catfish!

The car wash was a valuable experience. I had to show up on time, work hard, and practice plenty of self-discipline.

After graduation, my only dream was to head for Florida the following spring and try out for a major league baseball team. That was exactly what I did.

It was tough, but I was given a chance. I played in the International League for twenty-five dollars a game. I kept saying to myself, *I've got the talent, and I'm going to make it. I just know it!*

But as the days and weeks passed, there weren't any solid offers. *Well, maybe next year,* I consoled myself.

At home, my car wash job was waiting for me—yet my heart was still in baseball.

That fall, however, I damaged my knee while having fun at one of my other passions, motocross bike racing. When the accident happened, I knew in an instant: *There goes my knee. There goes my speed. There goes my baseball.*

Instead of another spring training on those fields of dreams in Florida, my future seemed tied with a rope to the car wash. Where else was I to go? At that point I was a young man without much of a future.

"Obnoxious and a Real Jerk!"

The woman who would eventually become my wife had enrolled in a local college, but because of an illness missed so many classes she decided to drop out.

That's when a friend asked her if she would like to take a job as a cashier at a local car wash. Needing an income, she quickly jumped at the opportunity.

So this is how Pam and I met. She was a good-looker and brightened up the day—not just for me, but for all the employees.

Her view of me, though, was somewhat different. As she describes it, "I thought Larry was obnoxious and a real jerk! In fact, I didn't want anything to do with him."

Let's face it: I was far from being a great catch. At that time in my life, I used foul language, drank too much, and was definitely rough around the edges.

But as the Good Book says, "The Lord works in mysterious ways."

In those days I was dating some other girls, but none had

the exceptional qualities of Pam. She was a supernice, sweet girl, and I wasn't used to that.

When we first started hanging out, there was a fellow who was interested in her, but I'm not sure if she trusted the guy. So on Friday and Saturday nights she would ask if I would tag along with the group. After a while, since we were spending so much time together, we realized that maybe we were meant for each other.

Pam and I dated for five years before getting married— we were both still working at the car wash. As she tells it, "I finally realized that deep down inside, Larry had a heart of gold and truly loved people."

I don't know how I deserved her, but I thank God every day that Pam fell in love with me.

When I was promoted to assistant manager, then manager, I thought I had it made. It was all I knew, and I felt I was on my way. But the pay was small, and the future was not much on which to pin my hopes. But what were my options? This seemed to be my lot in life, and I was going to make the best of it.

I tried to look important, wearing a huge key ring on my belt. Security became crucial when we joined a corrections department program and had convicted felons working for us at the car wash. A van would drop the men off at 7:30 a.m., and I was responsible for those guys for the rest of the day.

By now I was making $320 a week take-home pay, but I was risking my life! One day, I walked into my assistant manager's office to find him on the floor being choked by a disgruntled prisoner who thought he wasn't being treated fairly.

I thought, *This is nuts!* Surely there must have been a better way to make a living.

*   *   *

I hung out with people who drank beer, burped, and played softball. After a game the guys would send their wives and girlfriends home, and we'd head to a bar where we sat around and bragged how great we were in high school or American Legion ball. Of course I would tell exaggerated stories of my spring training escapades in Florida. We thought they were the "glory days." The weeks and months drifted by, and I had no real direction in my life. I was on a path going nowhere.

At my job, I had been promoted to district manager of the car wash chain over four locations, and I was resigned to the fact that this would probably be my career. Between my income and Pam's take-home pay of $280 a week we were getting by.

What Did I Have to Lose?

In August 1980, just three months after we were married, a friend asked if we would like to take a look at a business opportunity. I didn't even think twice.

"Why not?" I responded. I knew deep down that no matter how long and hard I worked at the car wash, I had to face the fact that it would eventually lead to a dead-end street—even if I stayed there my whole life.

The presentation I was shown that night was simple. I could become an independent business owner, selling exclusive and national-brand products—items people use every day, such as vitamins and household supplies. There was a compensation plan that would reward my efforts and plenty of support to guide and encourage me along the way. Plus, if I built an organization of men and women working with me, it could produce a stream of income with effort.

I wasn't sure about having others join me, but when my friend said, "All a person can say is yes or no," that somehow clicked with me.

However, almost immediately, a tug of war began playing in my mind. It was as if I was hearing two voices: one cheering, *You can do this*, the other warning, *Stay where you are*. But I knew in my heart I could work for the car wash until they dragged me out feet first and still never own the business.

"Sign me up," I responded. What did I have to lose?

Financially, I knew that even with an opportunity to be my own boss, it wouldn't happen overnight, and I needed to keep working at my day job.

Nothing Else Mattered

During the next few weeks and months, because of what I was learning about this new enterprise, I became so excited for the future that nothing else seemed to matter.

I went to work every day and put in my hours, but my mind was spinning like a top.

Before long, every possible moment I was sharing the business opportunity with those I knew—and even those I didn't. From the beginning, my belief in the products and the strength of the organization gave me a determination to build a business that would change my future.

I was totally unfamiliar with the techniques of qualifying potential associates; mine was a shotgun approach, and I targeted anything that moved. What I lacked in strategy I made up for in enthusiasm!

For Pam, however, it was different. She saw a spark in my eyes but was personally too shy to get involved. To say she had a poor self-image is an understatement. Pam had been abused as a young teen and was living with shame. Her deep-seated problems were linked and layered—so much so that her confidence was shattered.

She would make excuses about why she couldn't go with me to share this new business. "I'm too tired." Or, "I've really got to stay home and do some cleaning." One excuse was as good as the next.

The truth was that Pam was absolutely terrified of speaking—not just in public, but sometimes one-on-one. The very thought would make her break out in hives!

I can still remember the nights I would whisper in her ear, "Pam, you are a winner. You can do anything."

Little by little, I was raising her self-esteem. Her belief was growing, and we were becoming a team.

As the days rolled by, I found myself reading self-help books, attending business events, and applying the principles I was learning to my daily life. Principles dealing with goal setting, personal development, team building, and more that we will discuss later in this book.

My optimism knew no bounds, and I threw myself headlong into building what I believed was our answer.

Nights, weekends, it didn't matter. My calendar was full, and the dream for my future became a burning fire. Then came a moment of decision.

I Had a Choice

I had been building my new sales and marketing enterprise for about two years when my boss at the car wash called me into his office. What he said caused me to stop dead in my tracks. "Larry, we need to put you on a new schedule, and it means you will be working every other night and every other weekend."

My heart sank. How could I build my dream if all my spare time was suddenly being yanked away from me? It was as if everything I had worked toward was coming to a halt.

He told me about a car wash location with problems that needed to be straightened out, and he let me know that would be part of my assignment. "I think you are the one to handle this situation."

Instantly, I responded, "I'm sorry. I can't do that."

My words fell on deaf ears.

"I have already talked with upper management, and you don't have a choice. Either take the new schedule or we'll have to fire you," he bluntly told me.

"Sir," I replied, "I *do* have a choice!"

He smiled. "I know you have a little business going on the side, but I also know you're not making enough at that to pay your bills." He thought he had me over a barrel. Looking him straight in the eyes, I said, "If I have to work every other night and every other weekend, I'll never be able to build my business. And anyway, my future is not in washing cars."

My answer seemed to startle him, and immediately he shot back, "Larry, don't you know I have to fire you?"

"I'll save you the time," I quickly responded. "I quit!"

He was shocked when I reached down, unlocked the ring of keys from my belt, handed them over to him, and repeated, "You heard it. I quit! I'm out of here!"

My decision was absolutely final. There was no turning back.

Logically, it made no sense. Here I was, a husband and father with serious financial obligations, yet I was walking away from my only steady source of income. My new business was just getting off the ground—but was far from producing the kind of money I needed to survive. I learned in a hurry that there was no "get rich quick" scheme.

In my heart and mind, however, it all made perfect sense. My dream for success as an independent business owner was growing by the day—and I wasn't about to spend my life drowning in a car wash!

A Little Chilly

If I was going to be successful, I had to put things in high gear and share my opportunity with as many people as possible. There was no time to waste.

In starting a venture of any kind, momentum is essential. But I had the extra pressure of creating enough income to replace the paycheck I had left behind.

One evening, shortly after I began my new enterprise, the phone rang at about 7:30. A friend in the business asked, "Do you think you can show the plan tonight?"

Without hesitation, I told him, "Just tell me the time. I'm ready."

"Well, the fellow gets off work at 11:30. How about 11:45 tonight at your place?"

Wouldn't you know it: just before they arrived, our heater ran out of kerosene and I didn't even have five dollars to run out and buy some more. I wasn't about to cancel the meeting just because I didn't have enough cash. No more excuses!

Pam was in the bedroom with an electric blanket, so I brought our little electric heater into the living room—but it was far too small to adequately do the job.

I prepared the best I could, even putting on a second layer

of underwear beneath my three-piece suit. Plus, I drank a few cups of hot chocolate to warm up.

When my associate and his friend arrived, I apologetically said, "I know it's a little chilly in here, but we'll be fine."

I set up a small whiteboard and began to diagram how the business worked. Then I began to explain how people would be interested because everybody needs some extra money. Plus, it's a great way to form new friendships and prepare for long-term financial security.

At first, the men were sitting a few feet apart on the couch. But it seemed that every time I turned around, they had moved closer together. Finally, they pulled the afghan from the back of the couch and wrapped themselves together.

At the end of my presentation I bravely asked the fellow, "If you decide to become an independent business owner making $60,000 a year and could travel anywhere in the world, where would you go?"

"Someplace warm!" he answered.

"Have You Been Drinking?"

Fulfilling my dream often meant driving long distances to present the plan and attend conventions.

One night I was returning to Raleigh at about two o'clock in the morning. It had been a long day, and I was really tired. Then, coming down a hill, my Mustang must have hit fifty-five miles an hour because it began shaking and swerving all over the road. It was like wheeling a shopping cart filled with bowling balls!

Suddenly, I saw a flashing blue light in my rearview mirror, and a patrolman pulled me over.

Shining a flashlight in my face, he asked, "Mister, have you been drinking?"

"No, sir," I told him truthfully, "I haven't had a drink in years."

He was puzzled. "I thought you were the worst drunk driver I had seen in weeks."

Once he spoke with me, he realized I had not been drinking.

I finally convinced the officer that the car had a mechanical problem and could not go over fifty-five miles per hour without uncontrollable vibrations. He let me go.

The challenges seemed almost overwhelming, but nothing was going to dampen my spirit or slow me down.

Our Only Answer

One of my darkest days was when Pam and I had made a commitment to attend a business rally in the organization, and we were doing everything in our power to scrape up enough money for the event.

From our landscaping business we had put together about $600 in cash that Pam was to deposit in the bank the next day. That evening we spent time writing out checks to several companies we owed and put them in the mail.

However, when my wife made it to the bank, the $600 was nowhere to be found. She absolutely panicked. The sympathetic teller went out to the car with her to search for the cash because she understood the dire situation we were in. But the money was never found.

To us, this was like losing $1 million, because every one of those checks bounced.

To this day, I don't know how we managed to keep our

word and attend that event, but even through our tears we knew we had to be there. We scrounged up every dollar and dime we could find. In the long run it was the only answer we could see to learn how to correct our desperate financial situation, and I was totally committed to doing whatever it took to reach our objective.

Pam wondered, "Will success ever happen for us? Will our circumstances ever change? Is it always going to be this way?"

Day after day, month after month, I reassured her: "Trust me. I know in my heart we are on the right path. What we have found is bigger than you can ever imagine. I won't let you down—I promise."

There were no more excuses for failure. We were going to live our dream. The question wasn't *if*, but *when*.

2

The Amazing Power of a Dream

You see things; and you say, "Why?"
But I dream things that never were;
and I say, "Why not?"
—George Bernard Shaw

If money was not an obstacle, how would your life be different? What would you provide for your family that you're unable to do now? What kind of car would you drive? Where would you vacation? Who would you help? How would you spend your time?

To be honest, when I first grasped the concept that I could be an independent business owner, I was over the moon! But I still had a difficult time with the idea of having a dream for my future.

In those days, I could see only a week or a month ahead. I was like an immature kid—wanting to play ball after work, caring far more about my batting average than my check-book. More concerned with what my friends thought of my slalom technique on water skis than how I was going to pay for the stereo I had just financed. I was preoccupied with how fast I could ride a dirt bike instead of how to be the best possible husband that I could be for Pam. I had priorities, but they were way off base.

The business wasn't my real challenge. It was something far more personal. I had to work on and build a new me! I was twenty-four going on seventeen!

We were living the existence of losers. Our friends had two things in common: (1) they were all good, caring people, but (2) they were all broke.

Looking back, the reason I was living paycheck to paycheck was because I was suffering from a condition I now know as "failure disease." Its symptoms were "excusitis" and procrastination.

The toughest part was getting strong enough to win the game of mental ping-pong that was playing in my head. I was faced with choosing between a potential or a pastime, between winning or wasting my time.

Dreams? What dreams?

When Pam and I were first married, I had practically no positive vision of the future and was pessimistic concerning the world in general. Perhaps I had watched too many newscasts or read too many headlines about crisis and conflict.

When the subject of starting a family came up, I told Pam, "I don't think we should have any kids. With this world in such a mess, why should we bring children into it?"

My wardrobe consisted of jeans and T-shirts. That's what I wore to work every day and how I was dressed the first time I was shown the business opportunity.

At our wedding, I not only had to rent a tux, but I didn't even own a suit to wear to the rehearsal dinner—I had to rent that, too.

John, the person who first told me about the new enterprise, commented, "You might want to put on a tie at the next meeting." It was more than a suggestion. He wanted the business to be represented well.

I thought for a moment and replied, "Well, I do have a clip-on."

"That will be okay," he said.

The clip-on was one I had been given when I had a part-time job for a pest control company. It was black, with a large red termite on the bottom—with an even bigger foot embroidered above the termite!

When John laid his eyes on it he begged, "Please don't wear that. I'll bring you one of mine."

He also suggested I wear a shirt with a collar. Thankfully, I had one of those.

When John came over for the next meeting I was almost too embarrassed to tell him I didn't know how to tie a tie, so he offered to help me. I couldn't believe I was twenty-four years old and another man was standing there showing me how. He was tall and I was short, so the end of the borrowed tie was so long it practicality came out my pant leg!

This Could Be Huge!

Every waking moment I was thinking of what my life could become if I jumped into this new venture with both feet and gave it everything I had.

I had shifted gears, and my mind was now on overdrive—

and my dreams were multiplying by the minute. I was no longer thinking of just paying the bills, buying a new dirt bike, and perhaps taking a vacation. *This could be huge*, I thought. My vision was stretching and growing—far beyond the small house we were renting.

At nights I had a hard time falling asleep. I was building a future in my mind. The picture I saw was in 3-D, so real I felt I could reach out and touch success.

My friend John, who first shared with me the business opportunity, came to our house twice. And on the second visit he left behind his board and easel. As he was backing out of our driveway—which didn't take but a second—I ran to the door and yelled, "John, you forgot the…" But he was already gone.

Looking back, I think he left it on purpose.

His taillights were barely out of sight when I walked over to the board, popped open the cap of the dry-erase marker, and started drawing out the plan I had seen—even though I really didn't have a clue what I was doing. But what a feeling it gave me—as if I had the world in my hands.

I was so exhilarated to be using that blue marker, I immediately called up my best friend. "Mike," I exclaimed, "you've got to get over here."

"Why?" he asked.

"I've got something I want to show you."

"When?"

"As soon as you can get here."

Mike said, "I can't come now, but how about Saturday?"

"Great," I responded.

So a couple of days later he dropped by the house, and the first words that popped out of his mouth were "Okay, where is it?"

"Where is what?" was my reply.

"Larry, we're best friends. Go ahead and tell me. Where's your new dirt bike?"

Since motocross was our mutual hobby, we were always trying to outdo each other with dirt or street bikes, whatever we were riding at the time.

"Mike, it's not a new bike I want to show you. Honestly."

"Well then, what is it?"

"My new business," I said, holding back my excitement and trying to sound as dignified as I could.

Mike began to laugh uncontrollably. "You? You have a business?"

"Yes, I really do," I tried to assure him.

He looked around our meager home and remarked, "You don't have a business!"

Of course, he had every right to doubt my words. He knew what my life was really like.

"Sit down," I told him. "I'm hooked up with a great guy from Wilson, North Carolina, and he's teaching me how to get started. This thing is really amazing. You can be your own boss and set your own hours."

After he calmed down, Mike said, "Okay, show me what you've got."

"Well, I'm going to tell you how you can become wealthy—" I began.

"Wait just a minute," Mike interrupted. "You borrowed twenty bucks from me last week and haven't paid me back."

"Give me a little more time and I'll get it to you," I promised, "but right now, please, you've got to look at this fantastic opportunity."

At that point I was a novice and knew practically nothing about the venture I had become involved with—and really had no idea whether it would work. But one thing was certain—I was on fire!

My enthusiasm was contagious, and Mike agreed to join me. I'm happy to report that today, many years later, he stuck with the opportunity and has become a tremendous success.

Fired Up!

Once I caught the vision that my tomorrow could be better than my yesterday, my dream became so real that I began sharing what I had found day after day, night after night. I spoke with everyone I could and went everywhere—mobile homes, apartment complexes, government projects.

My friend Mike was something else, having me show the business to all kinds of individuals—hitchhikers, even men on parole. This went on for months, and it seemed the meetings were going downhill. One night, as I was showing the plan in a run-down old house, a cockroach ran up my leg. Another time the door to the apartment where I was speaking was open and gunfire could be heard in the parking lot!

I finally told him, "No more. This is ridiculous. If you don't find a real person with a real job, a real car, a real house, and a phone number, I am not going to waste my time."

The next day, he called and told me, "Larry, I've got a great prospect."

I answered, "You'd better be certain. At the last couple of meetings I wasn't sure I was going to get home alive!"

We drove out of Raleigh and headed for the man's house. After a while, Mike indicated a side road and said, "Turn right here."

"This is a trailer park!" I exclaimed.

"Oh, that's just a minor detail," he answered, shrugging me off.

We drove past the double-wides and the neatly land-scaped yards and headed to the back of the park, near the edge of the woods. There stood an old, rusting trailer with pit bulls chained up underneath. The bare yard looked like it was full of chicken bones!

"Mike, what in the world are we doing here?" I said nervously.

"Well, technically, it's a house!" he replied.

"Where is his car?" I asked.

"It may be in the shop" was all he could muster for a reply. I found out the guy was a third-shift forklift driver at a food warehouse.

The trailer was perched on a slope, and the front door was at the high end—surely, he must have had another way to get in! There were some concrete blocks on the ground, but it seemed like we were knocking on the bottom of the door.

When the man opened it, he was wearing a white tank top with yellow boxer shorts—and I had to look straight up!

"How are you doing, sir?" I began.

"Oh, come right on in," he said.

I felt like asking, *Do you have a rope?* Or, *Can you give me a boost?*

I was dressed in a three-piece suit, and it was August. Of course there was no air-conditioning in that dilapidated trailer. It was stifling—worse than a sauna. I looked around, and there was velvet artwork hanging on the walls—Elvis, and dogs playing poker!

The couple had a newborn baby who was hungry. And Momma didn't want to sit in the back of the tiny living room. She pulled up a chair right next to the spot where I had set up my whiteboard and easel.

Glancing over at Mike, I shot him a look that said, *When we get out of here you're a dead man!* I could see the fear of God written all over his face!

Needless to say, it wasn't a successful evening.

I certainly didn't build our business in a luxury setting. One evening, at our rented house, we had a small get-together for some of our associates. As we were standing on our little porch attached to the back, the entire deck suddenly collapsed, and we all fell to the ground. Fortunately, no one was seriously hurt.

Later, there was a night to remember when a friend asked me to share the business with some of his buddies. That Thursday, about six people showed up, so I got prepared, made a quick bathroom stop, and was ready to start the meeting.

After the presentation, over cookies and soft drinks, I was mingling with those present and having a blast. I was thinking to myself, *We're finally getting somewhere.* When the socializing was over, I announced, "Good to see you guys," and headed out the door.

It was January, and there was a light freezing rain. But the second I stepped outside I felt a cold north wind rush through my pants. I lowered my eyes and saw that my zipper was all the way down! Horrified, I realized that my shirt-tail was sticking out a few inches.

Rather sheepishly, I crawled into my car and drove home. Immediately, I ran to the phone and called my friend who sponsored the presentation. "Great meeting," he exclaimed. "They loved it!"

"Yeah, but I've got to ask you a question."

"Sure. What it is?" he replied.

"Was my zipper down all night?"

"Oh yeah," he answered.

"And you knew it the whole time?"

"Oh yeah," he repeated.

"Well, why in the world didn't you tell me?"

"Larry," he said, "you told me never to interrupt you once you started showing the plan. I was just doing what I was told."

In successful sales operations there are specific plans and protocols to follow when introducing prospects to the new business. One of the key principles we were taught in our company by our trainers was to get through the whole presentation and then answer questions. Otherwise, it was easy to get distracted by a tangent and not get to complete our pitch.

A Nervous Wreck

After being introduced to an organization that had unlimited potential and being mentored by some of the most positive people I had ever met in my life, I was being trained by the best and was developing a wealth of product knowledge to share with customers and associates. Many times after an evening meeting, we'd get together with our team members for coffee and talk through what we each did that worked well and how we could improve the next time. Getting together and sharing these lessons had two benefits: we learned from one another, *and* we built strong friendships. I can't emphasize enough how important it is to meet with your associates, share your successes and, yes, your failures, too, so you can encourage one another and learn from one another's experiences.

My dream soon exceeded any sport or hobby. I actually

believed we could pay off our credit cards and buy a car with real air-conditioning.

It was a new world. I heard leaders telling me, "If your dream is big enough, the facts don't count." I found myself repeating the same words to others.

At home, however, I had some serious work to do. Pam let me do my thing, but it took quite a while before she was totally convinced that I had made the right decision for our future. Since she wasn't an active participant in the business, she found it hard to understand my enthusiasm.

When I quit my job at the car wash and took the total plunge in a new direction, she was a nervous wreck, wondering what was really in store ahead. Her level of involvement was doing the paperwork, since I was far from being a genius with numbers.

I kept telling her, "Pam, this will work. The day is coming when we won't have to worry about calls from a bill collector. We're going to solve our financial problems, pay every debt, and live like we were meant to. You just wait!" At the time, we were existing hour by hour, but I knew deep in my heart it would not be that way forever.

I was being encouraged by people who didn't make excuses. They were not only successful but were willing to share all the knowledge they had to help me become an achiever. Failures and setbacks are all part of the growing experience. It's not about how many times we fall down; it is about getting back up and moving forward. These folks inspired me with this kind of thinking. I wanted to be just like them, working harder and working smarter. They were excited about living their dreams, and that was the way I wanted to live, too.

I Tried to Calm Her Down

One night I came home and learned that Pam had been bombarded by an aggressive bill collector. We didn't have enough money to purchase an answering machine to screen the calls. So every time the phone rang she picked it up, hoping it was someone in our business calling to place an order.

Nine times out of ten, however, it was a guy on minimum wage screaming, "You owe the money—and if you don't pay, we are going to send you to jail!"

This really got to her—and when I walked through the door, she would get to me!

I tried to calm her down. "Honey, if we don't have the money, we just can't pay them right now. If it happens again, go ahead and hang up on them!"

Of course, Pam was much too polite to do such a thing, so she would listen to their threatening words, become emotionally drained, and dump all her frustrations out on me. This happened time and time again. She was falling apart at the seams.

I was home one evening and answered a call from a bill collector saying that we owed eighteen dollars a month. It was for a video recorder—and we were four months behind. The guy on the phone had his script: "If you don't pay this week we will send someone out to pick up the VCR."

I responded, "Mister, if you do you'll be disappointed because I sold it to a neighbor, and he's going to be mad that you want it back!"

I was wrestling with the pressure the best way I could, and it was tough on both of us. Finally, I sat her down and said, "Pam, I can't deal with all the problems outside the house and come home to you challenging me and taking sides with a bill collector. I know we owe the money, and I will repay every cent. You don't need to remind me. I feel it, too, but you have to decide: are you going to put faith in the bill collector or in what we are doing?"

Finally, the moment of truth came when I asked her, "Are you with me?"

Through her tears she said, "Let's do it."

This was a major turning point that sealed our future.

Pam began attending meetings with me—despite the fact that she owned only two ten-dollar dresses. One was red, and the other was blue.

Still shy, insecure, and indecisive, she would always ask me, "Larry, tell me—which one should I wear?"

The color made no difference to me, as long as she was by my side.

I had a low self-image, too, but covered it up in another way: by being bolder, louder, and more obnoxious than anybody else!

When Pam moved into my corner, a heavy burden was lifted, and I felt a new freedom. I could leave the house without any fear or guilt, worrying, *What is Pam going to think?* She became my full-time supporter, and in my mind I could see her in the background and hear her cheering, "Go, Larry, go!" She totally did an about-face.

In those early days, before the Internet changed the way merchandise moved, we had to take orders, fill out the paperwork, and tend to dozens of details.

One night, when I arrived home from a meeting at one o'clock in the morning, I walked through the door and knew immediately that the heater had gone out again. It was so cold I could see my breath!

Inside, I noticed a blue-and-white blanket hanging up in the opening between the living room and the kitchen. *What's going on here?* I wondered.

Was I ever in for a surprise. When I pulled back the blanket, there was Pam, perched at the table, doing her paperwork, as cheerful as could be. The door to the electric oven was open, and Tara, now a year and a half old, was bundled up by her side.

I felt like a heel, but at the same time was so proud of Pam. She wasn't complaining, "Why did you put me in this position?"

We were now both on the same page—and we shared a deep, abiding faith that we would not just survive, but succeed.

The jobs I took while launching a business of my own were necessary for survival. In the process I met some wonderful individuals.

When I was still working at the car dealership I was sitting at my desk one day, hoping for a customer to appear and reading a yachting magazine. Danny, another salesman, walked into my cubicle and, curious, asked, "What in the world are you reading?"

"Oh, this? It's all about yachts," I responded.

"Why are you reading that?" he said.

Calmly, I told him, "Because one day I am going to own one!"

With a smirk, he replied, "How are you ever going to own a yacht being a car salesman?"

This was my golden opportunity, so I posed this question: "Don't you ever think about other ways of making money?"

"Why do you ask? What are you doing?" Danny wanted to know. "Have you got something going on the side?"

Trying my best to stay composed, I let him know: "I'm hooked up with some very successful businessmen. A couple of them are multimillionaires, and they are teaching me what they have learned."

I had his attention, so I continued, "One is a twenty-eight-year-old attorney who doesn't have to practice law anymore, and the other is a retired city manager who is a graduate of North Carolina State." And I couldn't resist adding, "They make more money in one month than you and I do in a year."

When he tried to pooh-pooh my dream, I bluntly told him, "I really don't know you, but I do know them. So I'm not going to waste my time listening to your opinion."

"Well, I didn't mean to make you mad," he responded. "I know you are a good person, and I just want to keep you from getting burned by some shysters."

Again, I repeated, "You haven't met my friends."

The people I was working with were living demonstrations of integrity and success. These were the most positive people that I had ever been around in my life. They were committed to helping me be successful. And that became one of the most important lessons I've learned and applied in my business. In his best-selling book *See You at the Top*, Zig Ziglar says it best: "You can have everything in life you want, if you will just help enough other people get what they want."

The Ten-Year Return

For the next two or three weeks Danny would stop by my desk whenever we had a break or the showroom was empty. He was always pounding me with questions such as "Aren't you leading people down a garden path? By trying to grow your business, don't you feel like you are using your friends?"

"No," I retorted. "My sponsor is helping me make money—and if my friends want me to do the same for them, I will. If they don't, they can still be my friends—or not."

After a few weeks of this back-and-forth banter, Danny and I went to lunch in my Volkswagen Rabbit loaner car. On the way, I took a minor detour, pulled down a side street, and drove through the wrought-iron gates of a huge mansion, not saying a word. There was a luxury Mercedes parked in the driveway, and I drove as slow as I could so we could take in the view. It was an impressive place.

At lunch I let him know this was the home of a gentleman I was in business with. Then I asked, "Danny, how long have you been selling cars?"

"Oh, it's been about ten years," he told me.

"Well, the man who owns that mansion has also been in his business about the same number of years." Here came the kicker: "Who do you think has had the best return on his time and life? You or him?"

There was dead silence. In fact, there was no reason for him to answer. You could have dropped Danny's entire house in that man's living room.

Danny remained quiet until we returned to the dealership. Then he asked, "Larry, how does this thing work?"

I told him, "If you are serious, maybe I'll take you to a meeting and have someone show you." I knew full well he wouldn't listen to me.

That same night we went to a meeting, and he was hooked. He became an independent business operator and today has an extremely successful organization all over the country—and overseas.

His returns are still multiplying.

A Dream and a Future

If Pam and I had looked at this opportunity logically, there was no way we could have held on to our dream. In 1985, our entire income was less than $10,000—which was below the federal poverty line.

That Christmas, Pam gave me two white shirts so I could look presentable, and I gave her a new Bible. We bought Tara a teddy bear we had put on layaway, paying five dollars a week for a month.

Pam made my mom a Christmas ornament because we couldn't afford to buy one. She found a pine cone in the yard, added glue and dribbled on some red and green sparkles. I gave my dad a $1.99 coffee mug from a local restaurant called Biscuitville. But at least with that mug, he could use their drive-through window and always enjoy a free refill!

Things were bleak. There were months when our water was cut off because I couldn't pay the utility bill. The phone went dead when a check bounced. I had to borrow a car. But every time I started sharing my business opportunity, my problems seemed to vanish. My thoughts were suddenly elevated to a new level. I had a dream and a future.

I trusted the team who encouraged me and said it would work. I didn't dwell on the present but focused on the future, because that was where I was headed.

I've heard it said that dreams are like stars: you may never touch them, but if you follow them they will lead you to your destiny. Pam and I are living proof of this truth.

Opening Doors

I didn't care what menial jobs I had to do to put food on the table during our days of struggle. I knew our problems were temporary and that the black clouds of today would soon turn to bright sunshine. There was a new, driving force.

Besides mowing lawns, I cleaned gutters, washed windows, hauled trash out of people's yards—whatever it took to make ends meet.

At one point I sold sweaters out of my trunk. I would drive over to Rockingham, North Carolina, to a place that wholesaled high-fashion irregular sweaters for five dollars each—Christian Dior, Gucci, etc. I'd drive to beauty salons, golf courses, and banks, and sell them for fifteen or twenty dollars.

One day as I was showing the sweaters at a car dealership, I asked a man on the lot, "Who is the top salesman here?" By this time I was becoming bold as a lion in sharing my business opportunity. He pointed to a red-haired guy, and I headed straight for him.

"What are you selling?" the red-haired guy asked.

Putting the sweaters aside, I told him, "This is what I do during the day for pocket change. At night I'm in business with some very wealthy guys." Then I asked, "If you are this great at selling cars, you need to see what my friends are doing to make some serious money."

"Is it legitimate?" he asked.

"Of course," I replied.

"Well, I was just curious."

His name was Campbell, and his future was about to drastically change.

Seeing the Invisible

Friend, when you are at a crossroads between your job and your dream, always choose your dream. But make sure you latch on to one that outweighs your fears and doubts.

Take it from one who knows: you can become whatever you envision.

The famous painter and sculptor Michelangelo was driven by things he could not see.

Once, he was reading Old Testament scripture detailing the life of David. In his mind, he visualized what the king must have looked like, and he decided to carve a sculpture of David's likeness.

He found a slab of marble and knew it would be perfect for what he saw in his mind's eye. So he brought the stone to his studio and began to examine the marble carefully. He walked around it again and again, month after month, visualizing what it would become. He was only twenty-six years old.

People would ask him, "When are you going to start working?"

Michelangelo replied, "I've been working every single day—looking and studying this piece of marble, and I believe I am seeing things that nobody else can."

It took more than two years of intricate work, but chisel by chisel he carved a masterpiece. It was unveiled in 1504, and his *David* has become one of the greatest sculptures of all time.

From my personal experience, I am totally convinced that you can become whatever you dream. As Mark Twain is reported to have said, "Twenty years from now, you will be more disappointed by the things that you didn't do than by the ones you did do. So throw off the bowlines. Sail away from the safe harbor. Catch the trade winds in your sails. Explore. Dream. Discover."

Your list of excuses for delay may be a mile long. Tell yourself, *No more detours or regrets. It's full steam ahead!*

3

CHANGED FROM THE INSIDE OUT

Five years from now you'll be the same person you are today except for the books you read and the people you meet.

—Charles "Tremendous" Jones

It is vital to understand where you are before you can determine where you want to go. I soon learned that if I was to be successful in a business of my own, I needed to make some major changes—inside and out.

Those in leadership charged my batteries, encouraging me, "Don't let a day go by without reading something to develop your personal growth. You feed your body; now you've got to feed your mind."

Specifically, they recommended books such as those by Napoleon Hill, including *Think and Grow Rich*, *The Master-Key to Riches*, and *The Law of Success*. Other books that influenced me greatly were *The Greatest Miracle in the World* by Og Mandino and *The Friendship Factor* by Alan Loy McGinnis.

In these books and so many others, I learned principles of success that were never taught to me in grade school or high school. The words penned by Hill jumped right off the page: "Whatever the mind of man can conceive and believe, it can achieve."

Was this really true? Well, I was determined and on a mission to find out.

I also read that to achieve ultimate success I had to burn the bridges behind me, close the back door, and block any escape route. No more excuses! There was only one direction to go—and that was forward.

What I was absorbing was certainly resonating within me. I carried a ton of garbage from my past that needed to be burned before I could start thinking, believing, acting, and achieving true success.

My Eyes Were Opened

Just as I was launching my business, a friend loaned me a copy of a book titled *The Magic of Thinking Big* by David J. Schwartz, PhD.

He also offered me this bit of advice. "Let me recommend that you start by reading chapters 2, 12, and 13. If you want to read the rest, fine, but start with those chapters first."

I couldn't wait to begin. In chapter 2 I read, "The fellow who has gone nowhere and has no plans for getting anywhere always has a bookful of reasons to explain why. Persons with mediocre accomplishments are quick to explain why they haven't, why they don't, why they can't, and why they aren't. Study the lives of successful people and you'll discover this: all the excuses made by the mediocre fellow could be *but aren't* made by the successful person."

In chapter 12, these words jumped out at me: "Nothing happens, no forward steps are taken, until a goal is established. Without goals individuals just wander through life. They stumble along, never knowing where they are going, so they never get anywhere."

Then, in chapter 13, I discovered, "You are not pulled to high levels of success. Rather, you are *lifted* there by those working beside and below you. Achieving high-level success requires the support and cooperation of others."

When I finished those three chapters, I actually became mad. I was upset with my parents, my family members, and every teacher I had through twelve grades of public school. Why? Because not one of them suggested that I read this book—or anything like it.

You see, in the matter of less than an hour, my eyes were opened and I learned more about life, success, and winning than I ever thought possible. Why wasn't I taught these truths earlier?

To me, it felt like most of my schooling amounted to being taught one useless fact after another. Sure, there is a need to know history, math, and science, but how does a person apply these things in the real world? Today, I am convinced that once a boy or girl learns to read and write, it's time to start inspiring young minds with their potential. It is never too young to start dreaming.

Even in the elementary grades, I wasn't exactly thrilled with school. I smile when I think of how much I hated spelling bees. There were too many rules for this kid—like *"I* before *e* except after *c."* I was more of a "big picture" guy. If I got close to being right, that was good enough for me.

I dreaded the days when our teacher would announce, "Everyone come up and stand in front of the blackboard." It was as if I was on a firing line. If you spelled the word correctly you could stay up front. If you missed it, you'd have to walk all the way back to your seat and let the whole class know you were a moron—at least that was how I felt.

So I decided the next time there was a spelling bee I'd make a quick exit and be done with it. When it was my turn, the teacher said, "Larry, spell *cat*."

"K-A-T," I responded.

"That's incorrect. You will have to sit down."

No problem, I thought to myself. At least I was out of the line of fire. It would have been worse if I had spelled cat with two *t*'s!

Looking back, I see how immature I was—acting like a smart aleck.

Classroom Questions

"What is pi squared?" my tenth-grade math teacher asked the class.

I raised my hand and blurted out, "Pop-Tart!"

Come to think about it, when is the last time you used pi squared when placing your order at a McDonald's drive-through or in aisle nine at the grocery store?

I also remember when we had a substitute teacher in our twelfth-grade psychology class. He asked us to write, in five hundred words or less, "Why This Desk Doesn't Exist."

About ten seconds later, I walked up front and handed in my paper.

"Mr. Winters, that was rather fast," he said.

"I'm finished," I told him, and returned to my seat.

He was rather surprised when he looked at the paper. I had written, "What desk?"

As you can imagine, I didn't get a good grade.

Eliminating the Junk

As part of building my new business, I began to seriously control what was going into my mind. I stopped watching the nightly television news. Why? Because the lead stories are based on doom, gloom, and all things negative. As they say in the news media, "If it bleeds, it leads."

In order to keep a positive and motivated outlook, I started screening what I listened to, what I saw, what I read, and who I associated with. I had to quit hanging out with many of my old friends. I didn't need to constantly hear "You can't," "Why are you wasting your time?" and "I know a fellow who went broke doing what you're doing."

Oh, they were still my friends, and I smiled and gave them high-fives when I bumped into them, but it was obvious they were essentially pulling me down, not building me up.

These were necessary and sometimes painful steps I had to take to rid my mind of junk and change my thought process. At first, it wasn't easy or convenient. Because of the decision I had made, there were certain individuals I no longer related to. I was becoming a new person, and they couldn't understand why.

My listening habits changed dramatically. I turned off and tuned out the radio disk jockeys who were spinning records with questionable lyrics and endlessly promoting products. Now I was popping in cassette tapes, and later CDs, of great inspirational speakers and motivators. They had so much to tell me.

In fact, I loved listening to these business leaders while driving to and from meetings more than anything I had ever done. Even today, after all the success we have achieved, I look back at these exciting days of building our business with fond memories. I was growing intellectually and spiritually, and developing leadership qualities that would shape my future.

My "Heart" Problem

My real transformation, however, involved much more than digesting positive material or hanging out with optimistic people. I had a "heart" problem—and didn't know it. No, it wasn't a health issue, but there came a moment when I realized there was an emptiness deep inside me that had never been filled.

Sunday morning, November 1, 1981, after fourteen months in our new business, there was a dramatic turning point. Pam and I were attending a leadership convention at the Hyatt Hotel, in Knoxville, Tennessee.

From the moment I became involved in our new venture, I began noticing something unique about the leaders. At first it was hard to pinpoint; then I realized I never heard foul language coming out of their mouths, and they treated everyone with tremendous respect. It soon became obvious that these people not only enjoyed a different lifestyle, but had a special something in their hearts I didn't have.

The trip to Knoxville was about the fourth such event Pam and I had attended. As usual, after the business sessions on Friday and Saturday, it was announced that there would be an inspiration hour on Sunday morning. It wasn't an official part of the agenda, but those who wanted to attend could do so voluntarily.

I had been to one of these Sunday morning meetings before, but nothing that was being said made much sense to me. It was like trying to understand Chinese arithmetic. So I slept through the next two.

This time, however, it was different. I had been building my new enterprise, yet nothing seemed to be going right. My life was a mess—and so were my finances and relationships. I was broker than broke!

I Listened Intently

On that Saturday night, I heard a man on stage announce, "Please come tomorrow morning, because I'd like to tell you my secret—what really matters to me and what caused me to succeed."

Since I was hurting inside and tired of losing, I awoke the next day and rode the elevator down to the ballroom. There were approximately eight hundred registered for the weekend convention, and at least six hundred showed up that Sunday morning. The room was set up with round tables of ten each.

I sat and listened to a highly successful man who had reached the place in life where I wanted to be. Because of his credibility and how he dealt with people, he had my undivided attention and I listened intently.

The "answer to life" he presented was simple—and one I had been around constantly. Yet I had never really heard or accepted the truth. He offered me the gift of God's Son, and I was ready and willing to receive it for the very first time.

It was truly a "come to Jesus" moment, and my heart was forever changed.

This gift was free—something I couldn't earn or work for. And when I realized the true value of what was being offered, I thought, *Larry, you're crazy if you don't accept this awesome gift.*

That morning, I made not only an emotional decision but a rational one—a commitment of how I was going to live my life from that moment on. Old things passed away, and everything became new.

I will always be grateful to the person who shared the simple but transformational message with me in Knoxville.

Story Time in South Jersey

Being "turned on" by divine principles was a far cry from how I was raised.

There was a set routine at our house on Sunday mornings when I was a kid, living on Williams Terrace in Runnemede, New Jersey. Mom and Dad would drop us off at Sunday School while they went to a nearby diner for breakfast. Then they'd pick us up, since none of us actually went to the morning church service.

What I looked forward to most was the story time. Our teacher was a rough, six-foot-two, tough construction worker from South Jersey. I learned about Noah and the Ark, David and Goliath, and how the three Hebrew children were thrown into the fiery furnace, but I can't remember any emphasis on how it applied to my life.

In the late 1960s, when I was old enough to attend church services on my own, my main interest was sports. So John, Rick, and some of my Catholic friends convinced me to go to Mass with them on Saturday evenings so we would have Sunday totally free to play ball. It sounded good to me. Even though I wanted to go to my own church on Sundays, the pull of sports was number one at the time.

At that time, we were into tackle football. No helmets, of course. We played teams our age from nearby towns— Barrington, Glendora, and Bellmawr.

The Mass was still in Latin, so I had no real understanding of what they were talking about. To be honest, I wasn't really comfortable because I didn't know how to act. I was always standing, sitting, and kneeling at the wrong times!

However, I loved the parish's athletic program and soon was on the local Catholic Youth Organization's basketball and baseball teams.

At home, there was no real moral compass and few limits or boundaries. Dad's advice was "Son, be careful what you do and don't embarrass the family." He didn't want me involved in any trouble that could cause him to lose his home or gas station.

Although I went to Mass, I was living without many guidelines. Nothing changed in my heart. My friends and I walked out of that Catholic church the same as we went in—and continued living as we had before.

After my freshman year of high school, in 1973, when Dad announced we would be moving to North Carolina, I begged and pleaded, "Please, let me stay here." I couldn't stand the thought of leaving my buddies.

"Well, if you want to sleep in a cardboard box and scrounge for your own food, fine. But we're heading south," my father bluntly told me. With great reluctance, I packed my bags and climbed in the car.

In our new location I started making friends and visited

several churches of different denominations with them. It was all confusing. One church denounced instrumental music, and I was told, "Music is of the devil."

At another a guy was on the platform playing a guitar. I said to my friend, "I thought music was of the devil."

He informed me, "Acoustic music is okay, but not electric guitars." Evidently the devil comes into the church through the wiring!

The next congregation wouldn't allow drums. "If you start pounding drums you wake up the demons!" they explained to me.

When Pam and I started dating we went to the church her parents attended. I really loved it, but nobody ever asked me, "If something were to happen to you, where would you spend eternity?"

I was twenty-four years old and had never been confronted with that question—ever. All my life I had embraced everything to the max, whether it was skiing or bike racing. I lived on the edge, and there had been far too many close calls to remember.

When I was in Florida playing ball, I was totally out of control. The weekends were for partying and drinking until I was practically out of my mind. I look back and wonder how I ever survived—the trucks on the highways I missed by inches, the cars I almost plowed into.

I certainly wasn't thinking about my soul, or eternity.

Just before we tied the knot, Pam's pastor called us to his office for a counseling session. He asked me, "Are you a Christian?"

"Yes," I answered without any hesitation.

"That's wonderful," he exclaimed. "Marriage is hard enough, but at least your faith won't be an issue." In truth, I was no more a Christian than I was a Cadillac. A person can profess to be something all day long, but saying you are and being one are two entirely different things.

Why did I say I was a Christian? Because my parents told me I was. In my heritage I had a Jewish grandfather and a Catholic grandma, but my mom and dad said our family was Christian, and that was that!

When I stood at the altar and repeated the wedding vows, I may as well have been quoting something out of *Mad* magazine. To me, the marriage process was something I had to go through so I could have a honeymoon.

Inside the Pages

What happened on that Sunday morning in Knoxville was by far the most important decision of my life.

Since my earliest days I respected God's Word, but I had spent practically zero time reading the Bible. Now, bursting with curiosity and hungry to know more, I couldn't wait to get my hands on one to read what it had to say.

Please understand, the reason I am relating this story is because it is such a pivotal part of my turnaround, both spiritually and in my new business.

In our large organization we are blessed to have people from all religious backgrounds: Jews, Catholics, and practically every Protestant denomination you can name. And now that our business has expanded worldwide, there are men and women from faiths I have never heard of.

Some may try to ignore the spiritual aspects of life and success, but I only know and can share what happened to me. As I like to say, a man with an experience is never at the mercy of a man with an argument.

Putting the Pieces Together

Life is much like a jigsaw puzzle with hundreds of pieces. In most cases we can look at the picture on the box top and figure out where certain parts will go.

However, many have never seen a clear picture of the puzzle. Perhaps your parents, teachers, or others never really painted the scene. Or maybe they did, but you didn't pay attention or you forgot what it looked like.

If you don't have the vision or the clarity, you will keep asking, "What am I trying to do here?" You may get a few edges linked together, but after a while you are picking up pieces and have no idea where they fit. So you slow down, lose interest, and eventually may even stop trying. As a result, you never find out what the finished picture is supposed to look like.

In some cases the puzzle is half completed, then a person comes along and knocks the puzzle off the table. Not wanting to start over, you give up altogether.

It was only when I made a heart commitment and became transformed on the inside that everything started to come into focus. The changes were amazing. I had a terrible temper that completely vanished. I stopped drinking immediately and have not touched alcohol since. I was hard-hearted, but soon began developing a love for others. In addition, I had never wanted children because I thought the world was too evil and didn't want to expose them. But then I began to see the goodness in people, and today we have an amazing daughter and two wonderful sons who are all such a blessing.

The ragged outline of the puzzle turned into a real picture. Over time, it went from black-and-white to color, and eventually I saw every small detail. Earlier this wasn't possible because I didn't have eyes to see or ears to hear. I was groping in the dark and could not see the truth, even though it was all around me.

Pam and I were married, but we had no compass, no map. We were just making things up as we went along. Oh, we had great parents who instilled a few dos and don'ts, but there was no coach, nobody calling the plays.

Thankfully, with God's help that all changed—not just for me, but also for Pam.

Unexpected Surprises

We knew we were on the right path by the way we handled the adversity we faced. Even though we were still struggling financially, there was a peace in our hearts that we were not walking alone.

Trying to make ends meet and help finance our new business, Pam and I would collect aluminum cans and take them to the recycling station for a little extra cash. At times there were unexpected surprises. For example, we were driving home on a brisk October morning as the sun was rising. We were looking for cans among the leaves that were piled on the sides of the road when suddenly both of us—at the same time—saw what looked like cash. We stopped, and lo and behold there were four five-dollar bills wrapped together. To us it was like $2,000.

If you were walking by with a magnifying glass, you'd probably miss them, but there they were. God was supplying our needs. This happened more than once.

"How's Your Business Going?"

Once, Pam was knee-deep in a Dumpster collecting cans—and there were bees flying all around her. To her amazement, she found four twenty-dollar bills, all wadded up.

That same day, two of Pam's old high school friends who worked in a high-end clothing store walked by in their preppy golf outfits. They knew we were starting a business because we had asked the women and their husbands if they were interested. They had told us no—and now they saw us sweating, rummaging through a Dumpster and tying plastic bags of cans on top of our beat-up car.

You can imagine how we felt when they asked, "How's your business going?"

I had to bite my lip, but it deepened my resolve to succeed if it took the last breath I had. Fortunately we were growing in our faith, and we claimed the words of the New Testament writer James the Apostle when he said, "Consider it pure joy...whenever you face trials of many kinds, because you know that the testing of your faith produces perseverance. Let perseverance finish its work so that you may be mature and complete, not lacking anything."

No lack! That was the place we were headed toward.

Take Control!

This journey of the reeducation of my mind and spirit became absolutely life-changing.

I was told early on by business leaders that what you read and what you listen to is actually your "scrimmage," so that when you are dealing with a real person you are "game ready." In other words, it's far better to blow it during a practice where nobody is keeping score than in a live game when it really counts.

Instead of concentrating on technique, I became hungry for information that would develop my attitude, thought process, and belief system. The average person has no concept of their potential and rarely achieves one-tenth of what they are capable of. From the books I devoured I learned that what enters your brain—and how—determines what comes out. Here was the most important factor: we *can* be masters of our own thoughts and control what enters our thinking.

If you carefully choose what to feed your mind, you will eventually see a dramatic turnaround. The positive will overwhelm and push out the negative, and your newfound belief will start being demonstrated in your behavior.

So I put a filter on my senses. I became extremely protective of what went into my ears—who I listened to and took advice from, whether at work, my motocross friends, the baseball team, even relatives. Suddenly I was in control, and the success principles I was learning found fertile soil in which to grow. And to this day I am passionate about feeding my mind the most nutritious food I can digest.

When you take ownership of your thinking and your attitude, you suddenly become the captain of your future. As a result, all the criticism in the world is not going to deter you from your goal.

"These Words Are for You"

Today, I tell everybody to do whatever it takes to plant good thoughts into their mind at least fifteen minutes a day. I believe even the busiest person can carve out at least that amount of time.

For me, I read every night before I fall asleep—and I have done this consistently for years. You might be a sunrise person and want to read before you start your day.

I did not begin reading to impress anyone or gain anybody's approval. It was because I personally became excited about the prospects of success and realized that it was absolutely necessary for me to change and grow into the person I needed to be.

Many nights I can't stop turning the pages after only fifteen minutes. I become so engrossed that I read for thirty minutes, an hour, or even longer. More than once it seems that God Himself is speaking to me: *These words are for you. Learn them. Apply them.*

There were times in those early days when I read until four o'clock in the morning—yet still had to be at the car wash by 7:00 a.m. The hours didn't matter.

Before my transformation, I would party all night and still somehow show up for work. I had been on drinking binges with the best (or worst) of them and didn't get any shut-eye. But now, even though I was still losing sleep, I was energized. I was feeding my mind, my soul, and my spirit. I'll let you decide which choice was best.

It is impossible to fully explain what a profound difference this has made in my life. For example, I was always a taker by nature. I became a giver by trying to help others both inside and outside my business. In my early days, I never gave to the church—or anybody else, for that matter. But now, sharing my blessings with others not so fortunate is one of my greatest joys.

I am such a strong believer in reading and absorbing books and CDs that are filled with encouragement, positive reinforcement, and proven, godly principles because it builds and fortifies your faith—faith to become the dynamic man or woman you were born to be.

"Wait for Me!"

Pam's journey of personal growth paralleled mine—and in many respects surpassed it. She was reading, applying, and gaining self-esteem at an amazing pace. It was no longer just "Larry" who could help and encourage people through his God-given talents and abilities. She could do it, too.

At first, when I was spending considerable more time in self-help material, in my mind I was thinking, *Hurry up, Pam. You need this.* However, once she delved into the substance of things, she left me behind—like a one-legged man in a hundred-meter dash. Now I was saying, "Not so fast! Wait for me!"

But public speaking was so painful for her that people couldn't help notice her discomfort. When Pam began sharing her thoughts with audiences, there were those who took me aside and asked, "Why did you make her do that?"

The truth was that Pam really desired to overcome her fear and was willing to try. I watched her grow from being so frightened she could hardly see straight to becoming the articulate, powerful, amazing speaker she is today.

Enjoy the Process

One of the principles I discovered was not to get uptight and overanxious when there were reverses in my progress—and there surely were. When you come to the realization of who you are and have total confidence in your plan for the future, relax and enjoy the ride.

Yes, it's essential to be focused and have a sense of urgency, but make sure there is joy in the process. This is vital if you are building a team of people who are involved in reaching goals. When you are relaxed, others will automatically be drawn to you.

I will always remember going to my American Legion baseball games and never knowing if I would be a starter. I was one frustrated ball player! On the field I would have good games, average games, and bad games. Even though I exerted my best effort, my self-confidence as an athlete vacillated up and down like a yo-yo.

One evening, the team manager called me over and said, "Son, you've got plenty of tools, but you are never going to hit a lot of home runs. You have a great glove, and you are as fast as a gazelle. They can't strike you out—and if you get on base you are an automatic double or triple. But you've got to relax." He continued, "Larry, you are trying too hard."

"Well," I told him, "I just want to make you proud and do well for the team. My goal is to earn a starting position."

He hesitated a moment, then responded, "Here's what I have decided to do. I am going to name you as my starter in center field, win, lose, or draw. I don't care what the other coaches or parents say. Because of your age, you've got two years in this league—the rest of this season and all of next year to be my starter." Then he added, "You don't have to win the position, you've got it. So it's your spot to lose."

He added, "I want you to come to the park knowing you are going to be in the game, so relax and just play ball. You're my guy. You can't prove me right, but you can prove me wrong, so just go out there and have fun."

Wow! Those were the words I needed to hear. My batting average improved and so did my on-base percentage and stolen bases. I became a much better ball player. Why? Because I was no longer walking on eggshells. I was no longer trying to fit in.

Before every game, I was thinking, *I'm the starting center fielder and the leadoff hitter—win, lose, or draw.*

When I batted 0 for 3, I didn't go home worrying, *I hope I play Tuesday night.* When I got picked off first base or thrown out at second, I didn't have to wonder, *Will I be playing in the next inning?*

You can't win with a mind cluttered with constant doubt: *Can I do it? Do I belong? Is this the right thing to do? Am I wasting my time?*

More Than a Degree

It makes no difference who you are, where you were born, or what your background is. You may be the most educated or the least educated person walking the planet, but this will not be the sole determination of your future.

While I am a strong advocate of education, it is futile to always equate success with academics. You can display more degrees on your wall than a thermometer; they do not guarantee—or indicate—personal achievement.

- Bill Gates, the founder of Microsoft, is a Harvard dropout. When he was invited back to speak at a commencement, he said, "I'm a bad influence. That's why I was invited to speak at your graduation. If I had spoken at your orientation, fewer of you might be here today."
- Steve Jobs, who created Apple Computer, the Mac, the iPod, and the iPad, quit his studies at Reed College in

Portland, Oregon, because of the financial hardship it placed on his working-class parents.

- A young man in Chicago named Walter dropped out of high school at the age of sixteen to join the U.S. Army. However, he was rejected because he was underage. So he decided to join the Red Cross and was sent to France, where he drove an ambulance before World War I ended. He had a knack for drawing cartoons and soon moved to Kansas City, but no one wanted to hire him. So he began creating some cutout characters that he transferred to film, and they were a hit in local movie houses. Walt Disney then moved to Hollywood, and the rest is history. Not bad for a kid who didn't make it through high school.

- Frank Lloyd Wright, the acclaimed American architect, dropped out of his studies at the University of Wisconsin after one year, only to spend his lifetime designing some of the most admired buildings in the world.

- When you see great movies such as *Titanic* and *Avatar*, it's hard to believe that Oscar-winning director James Cameron dropped out of Fullerton College, a two-year community college in California. He married a waitress and became a blue-collar worker, driving buses for the local school district. In 1977, he saw *Star Wars* and had a dream to make films like that. It wasn't a dream for long!

Think of these acclaimed people who didn't finish high school: George Bernard Shaw, John D. Rockefeller, Peter Jennings, Tommy Lasorda, and thousands more.

Cornelius Vanderbilt, the railroad magnate and one of the wealthiest Americans of the nineteenth century, had very little formal schooling and was considered illiterate—until he became too wealthy to ignore.

What's Holding You Back?

I heard the story of a man who was a janitor at St. Peter's Church in London. But because he couldn't read or write, the minister of the church fired him.

Down through the years he had saved up enough money to start a small business—and decided to venture out and open a tobacco shop. It was such a success that he opened another, and another, until he had stores dotted all over London—making tremendous profits.

One day he sat down with his banker, and the financial executive said, "What you have accomplished is truly impressive. Just think how far you would have gone if you had learned to read and write."

The illiterate entrepreneur looked at him and replied, "I'd still be a janitor back at St. Peter's!"

What Are You Feeding Your Mind?

Your brain is a priceless gift from God. It is irreplaceable, limitless, and your most valuable possession. How foolish to waste it. Begin to examine *what* you learn—and how it will shape your future.

Memorizing facts nobody cares about is cool if you want to be a contestant on *Jeopardy!* or win a trivia game. But this won't result in financial freedom.

Your mind can be programmed for failure, mediocrity, or success. Like a computer, it is receiving data from what you think, feel, taste, touch, see, hear, and read. Everything is there—ready to be recalled in a split second when needed.

Since it is your decision-making process, I believe you

need to expand your mind with the most positive, optimistic, ethical, inspiring material possible. When you do, the choices you make will not only be rewarding for you but will benefit every person who is touched by your life.

William H. Danforth, in his classic self-help book *I Dare You!*, says, "When you read a book, don't let the author do all your thinking for you. Stop at the end of that sentence or page or chapter which 'brings you up with a start.' Interpret these thoughts into something definite in your own life. How can you apply it in your work tomorrow?" And he adds, "Venture courageously into new mental realms. Think originally. If you can contribute one ounce of original thought, if you can originate just one new idea, you have dared well."

This is advice worth putting into practice.

A Real Life Lesson

The following rules are adapted from an article by educator Charles J. Sykes titled "Some Rules Kids Won't Learn in School."

Rule #1: Life is not fair—get used to it.

Rule #2: The world won't care about your self-esteem. The world will expect you to accomplish something *before* you feel good about yourself.

Rule #3: You will *not* make $40,000 a year right out of high school.

Rule #4: If you think your teacher is tough, wait till you get a boss. He doesn't have tenure.

Rule #5: Flipping burgers is not beneath your dignity. Your grandparents had a different word for burger flipping—they called it Opportunity.

Rule #6: If you mess up, it's not your parents' fault, so don't whine about your mistakes, learn from them.

Rule #7: Before you were born, your parents weren't as boring as they are now. They got that way from paying your bills, cleaning your clothes, and listening to you talk about how idealistic you are. So before you save the rain forest from the parasites of your parents' generation, try delousing the closet in your own room.

Rule #8: Your school may have done away with winners and losers, but life has not. In some schools they have abolished failing grades and they'll give you as many times as you want to get the right answer. This doesn't bear the slightest resemblance to *anything* in real life.

Rule #9: Life is not divided into semesters. You don't get summers off and very few employers are interested in helping you find yourself. Do that on your own time.

Rule #10: Television is *not* real life. In real life people actually have to leave the coffee shop and go to jobs.

Rule #11: Be nice to nerds. Chances are you'll end up working for one.

Life's More Than a Job

The words of Charles Sykes should be a wake-up call, not only for young people, but for *all* people. The message I draw from them is that the workaday world is not the most exciting place to spend your future. It is one more reason that I am devoting my life to showing men and women how to build a business of their own and becoming financially free.

What I witnessed in the first few years of starting my own enterprise was a dramatic change in me. There was an about-face in my outlook on life and in my relationships with others. I was being a better husband and father. My negative habits were becoming a thing of my past.

The words I spoke changed. I began appreciating things as never before. I was more loving and encouraging, and I had a stronger belief in people.

Not everyone may have noticed, but I sure knew the difference. I was consciously putting into practice what I was reading and hearing from inspiring, motivated leaders who had proven their own success.

Now I am asking you to make a commitment to change—from the inside out.

4

Success Is a Planned Event

Good fortune is what happens when opportunity meets with planning.

—Thomas Edison

Let me clue you in on a little secret. Success doesn't jump up and attack you. It's not just floating around in thin air and all of a sudden—BAMM! What was that? I just got hit with a $300,000-a-year income!

If you drift through life thinking moving to Easy Street is attributed to pure luck or the result of being in the right place at the right time, you're living in a fool's paradise. Those who believe that winning is haphazard will waste precious years waiting to get hit with it—whatever "it" is. This just doesn't work.

However, when you wake up to the realization that true success is a designed, programmed event, and you begin following the plan to make it happen, you are well on your way to the top. This is a secret many overlook, yet it is a proven key to ultimate success.

Whether it is in the field of merchandise, medicine, or ministry, the same principle applies. You copy the tried-and-true pattern of those who have achieved. No experimenting or detours.

More Than Luck

Sorry to burst your bubble, but winning the lottery isn't the answer, either. I've actually heard people say, "If I can somehow just pick the right numbers, all my problems will be over."

Far from it. The trail of men and women who have won multimillion-dollar jackpots is littered with tears and tragedy. Why? Because they weren't prepared and couldn't handle their sudden windfalls. The failure rate is high—yes, there may be a rush of temporal pleasure, but it is often accompanied with long-term pain.

- A woman in New Jersey won the lottery *twice*, for a total of $5.5 million. Sadly, she was a heavy gambler and lost it all in the casinos of Atlantic City. Today she lives in a trailer park and is flat broke.
- A man who won a $16.2 million jackpot in the Pennsylvania state lottery was sued by an ex-girlfriend for a share of his winnings—and she won. His brother hired a hit man to try and kill him, hoping to inherit some of the winnings. Other relatives bugged him constantly for money. Within one year he was $1 million in debt

and had to file for bankruptcy. He now lives on food stamps and has a small monthly stipend.

- A young man in England won a jackpot worth the equivalent of $1.9 million. He spent it all on a trip to the Canary Islands, a wedding, and a house. A year and a half later, after blowing it all, he was forced to take a job flipping hamburgers.

When I was in my early twenties, I was earning a meager salary at the car wash. I shudder to think what would have happened if I'd suddenly started making $4,000 a week. If a person doesn't know how to handle a small amount of money, a sudden influx of cash just compounds the problem. Without absorbing what I learned in the process of developing my business, I would have never been able to cope with the wealth that was waiting in the wings.

Success rarely happens overnight—and for me it was a drawn-out journey. But I put the principles of goal setting, personal development, teamwork, and leadership I had discovered into practice, and over time the pieces fell into place. Along the way my priorities changed, and I was ready for the responsibility of managing wealth when it arrived. I now thank God it wasn't instantaneous.

Start Flying

To lift a giant Boeing jet from the tarmac takes a whole lot of energy. In fact, an airplane uses much more power to get off the ground than when it's soaring effortlessly above the clouds.

It took us six years to finally gain our momentum and become financially free. But for Pam and me, they were the most life-changing, growth-producing, necessary years of our lives. It wasn't until 1989 that we passed the six-figure mark in income.* And that was just the beginning!

Others have reached similar goals in less than half that time, but since we had so many negative patterns to break it took longer. The number of months or years is not as important as what happens in the process.

Was it worth the journey? Without question.

You've Already Won!

It was as if I had been awakened from a coma when I finally realized that success was a choice, not a happenstance. However, plenty of mental adjustments were required before I started following a time-tested system and making better decisions.

I had to learn to think positive rather than negative. However, there is more to the process than most people realize. For me, it required having the vision and clarity to see opportunities in all circumstances. I stopped focusing on what was wrong with people and started seeing what was good about them. Plus, I was putting into daily practice the advice I learned in the books I was reading by other successful leaders.

If it is your goal to reach the top rung of the ladder, let me give you this advice: start treating your opportunity as a business. Take it seriously. If you consider it a hobby, I can guarantee it will be an expensive one. And if you think it's a social club, it will cost you dearly.

I've met those who talk a big game and brag about their talents and abilities, but they fail to do what it takes to build a solid enterprise.

So when you are ready to climb to the level of a high achiever, make certain that every aspect of your venture is operated on solid business principles. Examine every detail carefully.

Success is a duplicable pattern—and so is failure. This is why it is essential to study the actions of true winners. When you learn what they know, think as they think, do what they do, and say what they say, it won't be long until you'll be holding a funeral for failure.

I tell people again and again, "You've already won," because if you link your future to a proven plan and are committed to perform what is required, success is inevitable. It's automatic.

Steps to Success

There are several steps necessary for personal and professional achievement.

STEP #1: *Here is an extremely important detail: take the time to make sure the process you are involved in is duplicable.**

History provides plenty of examples. Henry Ford was not successful only because he was able to build a gasoline-powered automobile; there were several others in his day who achieved the same goal. However, Ford had a vision to mass-produce every individual part of his Model A and set up an assembly line that resulted in hundreds of thousands of cars. It changed transportation forever.

This duplicable pattern has proved successful for thousands of enterprises, from hotel chains to tax preparations services and direct marketing companies. The Policies and

Procedures Manual is a guideline to be followed to achieve your goals.

STEP #2: *Success requires total commitment—of your time, thoughts, energy, and finances.*

I've been asked, "Larry, how do you know if a person is really committed? What is the evidence?" In my experience, if somebody is totally committed to building his or her business, they aren't distracted by lesser priorities; they are focused on working until a task is completed, and they don't settle for doing anything less than their very best, every day.

STEP #3: *Demonstrate a persistent and consistent effort.*

This is where the pattern for success comes into play. Being persistent means you keep knocking and knocking at the door of resistance until it opens. As Ralph Waldo Emerson once said, "A man is a hero, not because he is better than anyone else, but because he is brave for ten minutes longer."

It also requires being consistent—executing the same proven plan over and over until your business grows with more customers buying your products or services, more people working with you to serve those new customers, and, if you are conservative with your finances, your income will grow as well.

It is said that a bee will visit 125 clover heads to make one gram of sugar. If you multiply that, it comes to over three million trips for bees to make one pound of honey. That's the kind of persistence that each of us needs to have when starting and growing our business. Consistent attention to detail without being distracted is an essential principle for every small business owner to practice from day one.

STEP #4: *Be consistent and trustworthy.*

The reason the process of planned success works is because when you don't overreact to problems, and stay with the blueprint, you become predictable and people will learn to follow your leadership. If people see how you react in one situation they know this is how you will act in the next. In other words, you are emotionally stable and others can trust you.

Let's look at the reverse of this: if you are inconsistent in your reactions and leadership, people will have a harder time knowing what to expect and question whether or not your word can be trusted.

It's sad to see a man or woman whose life is operating like a Ferris wheel at the state fair. Their mood swings take them up and down, high and low. One day they are on top of the world, the next they are despondent and crying—you never know at which point you'll find them. This is why every person needs to take an introspective look at their emotions. If you are unable to harness your own feelings, how can you expect to be consistent enough to relate to others and build your future?

STEP #5: *There are two mortal enemies of consistent effort—distractions and struggles.*

Fortunately, you have the power to take charge of self-imposed distractions.

When Pam and I were dating and during the first few months of our marriage, we went to movies more times than I can count. Of course, softball came first. I played for three teams, nine to twelve games a week. I'd risk my life for a stupid fly ball so I could hear a few compliments back in the dugout!

Pam was always up in the stands—swatting mosquitoes
and watching me run around the bases with a bunch of
other twenty-five-year-olds. Good guys, but they certainly
weren't focused on tomorrow.

However, when I latched on to a business opportunity
that turned me on, my mind-set changed overnight. I threw
my self-imposed distractions overboard and became persistent and consistent in building my future.

In those early days, we even cut out going to birthday
parties unless they were for our immediate family. I came to
the decision that by immersing myself in growing my enterprise, the day would come when I would be totally free and
could attend all the birthday parties I wanted!

STEP #6: *Delayed gratification is essential if you are
determined to succeed.*

I asked myself, *How many multimillionaires play softball?*
As much as I thought, I couldn't name one.

I can clearly recall the time I told my coach, "I'm not
going to be on the team anymore."

"Larry," he pleaded, "you can't leave us now. We really
need you."

If something drastic had happened to me, whether a
health problem or an accident, do you think that the softball team would have supported my family for the rest
of their lives? The moment had come for me to make a
choice—and thank God I made the right one.

I once owned a T-shirt with these two words printed on
it: "NO FEAR!" In smaller letters it read, "If you're not living on the edge, you're taking up too much space." To me,
it was more than a clever slogan; it was the way I wanted
to live. I realized that since we only go around once in this

world, I would get out of it what I was willing to put in. So I wanted to see how far it could take me.

Let me encourage you to put these six steps into practice. It WILL change your life and your business!

Get Out of That Rut!

In the far north of Canada it's so cold that there are only two seasons—winter and July. When the back roads finally begin to thaw, they become so muddy that cars or trucks leave deep, embedded ruts. Then, before long, they freeze over and those ruts become a real challenge for drivers.

On one road, they erected a sign that reads: "Driver, please choose carefully which rut you drive in, because you'll be in it for the next twenty miles."

This also applies to our lives. We have to make sure of the path we decide to take. Once made, that choice can determine your destination.

It's Your Decision

I've met people who would much rather stay on their bowling team than temporarily give it up so they could do what it takes to really succeed.

Some people are so consumed with hunting that they have that "deer smell" on them—even after the season is over. Others spend their weekends with a fly rod and fancy lure, trying to catch that bigmouth bass.

Great! But is now the time? You may deeply love your passions, but I beg you to take seriously what I am saying.

You simply must put these things on the back burner and concentrate your total efforts on doing what it takes to build a solid, sustainable business of your own. Eliminate distractions. Focus on the work at hand. And one day in the not-so-distant future, you will have all the freedom you desire to live your dreams. Then you can fly to Alaska and hunt and fish until you run out of ammunition or bait.

Practically anybody can drive a $400-a-month car. It belongs to the bank. Maybe that's why they have drive-through windows—so every time you pull through they can take a look at their automobile!

I hope you understand that the only thing I am putting down is a "broke" mentality.

Sadly, most have been trained simply to do a job and get a check. It's been said that being broke is a temporary situation, but being poor is a state of mind. This is why it was necessary for me to change my thoughts before I changed my actions.

The world teaches short-term thinking. But if you climb on board with the right plan and follow the steps I gave you in the early part of this chapter, the time and effort you invest today will return to you beyond measure.

The Planned Event

When I was still at my day job building my dream, I didn't take my vacation time all at once. I took it one day here and there—so I could go where I needed to be. I dotted every *i* and crossed every *t*, and stuck faithfully to the plan that would bring my freedom.

Nothing was going to distract me or interrupt my steady advancement.

I became a student of the "planned event" called success—specifically as it involved the enterprise in which I was involved. I listened to the advice of winners, but I also learned what *not* to do from negative examples.

It's important to know that nobody forced me to do this. There wasn't a boss putting me in a headlock, demanding, "Either meet these goals or you're out of here."

One of the most exciting aspects about having your own business is that every day you can restart and reset. If you veer off course, you can look at the road map, retrace your steps, follow the instructions, and keep moving forward.

I didn't get hung up along the way or make excuses for why it wasn't growing as fast as I would have liked. I just wanted to make sure I was doing everything properly and heading in the right direction.

You see, it doesn't matter how long it takes you to be free. When you're free, you are free!

I look at the average person and wonder, *What's the hang-up?* This is something every person needs to consider. What bondage are they under that keeps them from saying, "I am going to work harder for myself than I ever would for a boss"?

A New Mentality

You can do yourself a huge favor by separating the relative simplicity of building a business of your own from the complexity of getting yourself on track.

Personal change usually involves getting rid of some old habits and overcoming deep fears you may have been clinging to your whole life. Since so many are living tangled lives, this may not happen at the pace you desire. In my case, being broke was no one's fault but my own. The fact I was in my midtwenties and living in a house that had nine hundred square feet wasn't because of the government, my parents, or my teachers. It was my own fault because of the way I thought.

Instead of an "abundance" mentality, I had a "lack" mentality. I could have operated in faith, but instead I chose "doubt" thinking.

Thoughts take on a life of their own, and people wind up exactly where they put themselves. But I can tell you from personal experience that if you want to change, you really can. As President John F. Kennedy once said, "Change is the law of life, and those who look only to the past or the present are certain to miss the future."

"This Is It!"

Commitment starts when you decide to dive into your opportunity headfirst. You don't timidly stick your toe in the water to see if it is hot or cold—or put your finger in the air to determine which way the wind is blowing. You begin by believing: *This is it! I don't care what anybody else thinks. I'm going for it!*

More than once I've met those who comment, "Well, I'm going to try this for three months. But if it doesn't produce what I think it should, I'm out of here."

Such a person should never waste his or her time trying. They have lost the battle before they even begin.

A Greater Cause

Later, as you get involved in the entire process and learn to trust your associates, the business plan, the products, the delivery system, and the financial rewards, your commitment will have roots and grow much stronger. This same basic set of principles applies to literally hundreds of enterprises and organizations in which you may choose to get involved.

Now you begin seeing a greater cause, a higher purpose, and an ultimate destiny. At first, you're not ready to embrace such a vision, but the more you mature and develop, the easier it becomes to see the entire picture. This is when life takes on a deeper meaning. You begin to understand why you were placed on this earth and the eternal impact you can have on others.

If you're totally committed and there is significance to your life, no road is too rocky and no hill is too steep. You can reach any destination. To me, it was simple—nothing more than looking at an opportunity and saying, "Yes, I can and I will."

Noted educator William A. Ward counsels, "There are four steps to achievement: plan purposefully, prepare prayerfully, proceed positively, and pursue persistently."

I wholeheartedly agree. I pray you want to do more with your life than pay a mortgage and work forty years—if they let you! There is no greater thrill than to climb out of the quicksand of mediocrity and to start making a difference in this world.

Break Free!

Some people waste their lives going around in circles.

An experiment was conducted with what is called "processionary caterpillars." These are worm-like creatures that travel in long lines at the same pace, giving no thought to their final destination. They simply blindly follow their leader.

A nineteenth-century French researcher, John Fabre, placed a group of these caterpillars on the rim of a large flowerpot. The leader was nose to tail with the last caterpillar in the slow, unending procession. It was impossible to tell who the leader was and who the followers were.

In the center of the flowerpot they placed a large amount of food. Well, the caterpillars paraded around the rim day in and day out, until after about seven days, they began to die off, one by one. Food was only inches away, within their reach, but they died of starvation and utter exhaustion. If they had only ventured outside their comfort zone and altered their habits, they would have survived.

Stay awake! Be aware of your surroundings and break free.

Tenth in Line

I heard the story of an up-and-coming young journalist who was anxious to begin his career. He saw a "help wanted" ad in his newspaper that seemed like the perfect opportunity. He phoned the paper and was told, "Be here at 10 a.m. tomorrow morning. That's when all applicants will be interviewed."

With his résumé in hand, he arrived early the next morning. However, he wasn't too thrilled to find nine other journalists standing in line ahead of him. So he took his place and looked over the competition. Then, after thinking about the situation, he took out a pen and wrote on a piece of paper. He walked up and handed the paper to the secretary, telling her, "It's very important that your boss reads this as soon as possible."

When the executive read the note, he broke out in a big

smile, anxious to meet the person who had written it. The note read: "Dear Sir, I'm the young man who is tenth in line. Please don't make any decisions until you see me. You will not be disappointed."

Because he believed in himself, he was hired.

Don't Negotiate the Price of Success

Focus, focus, focus!

Moving your business from the excitement level to productivity isn't that difficult when you have put the past in the rearview mirror and become focused like a laser on the task at hand. The moment you are willing to totally commit to a single purpose, you are no longer negotiating the price of success.

Gone are the nagging questions: "How much money will I have to invest?" "How many miles will I need to drive?" "How many presentations will I have to make?" That's negotiating.

Friend, you can't have your thoughts and actions divided between doubt and belief. There is a passage in the Bible that explains this perfectly: You must *"believe and not doubt, because the one who doubts is like a wave of the sea, blown and tossed by the wind. That person should not expect to receive anything from the Lord. Such a person is double-minded and unstable in all they do"* (James 1:6–8).

Oh, the power of a decision! I take my hat off to any individual who confidently says once and for all, "This is my future—my career!"

When you are able to utter those words from your heart, you have mentally turned the corner and are on the avenue called Achievement. Sure, you will encounter challenges along the way, but the journey eventually becomes easier because of the nonnegotiable decision you have made.

I Had an Advantage

Regardless of the entrepreneurial organization you choose to become a part of or the plan for success it offers, face the fact that not everyone is going to join your team. Every person is unique. One likes catsup on their fries and the other one doesn't. But I'm not going to stop eating catsup just because it turns another person off.

Don't get uptight about starting a business of your own that grows by others getting involved. It's either interesting to them or it's not. There are millions of people in this world, and you want to grow with those who are hungry for success.

I learned early on that if a man or woman didn't want to partner in business with me, it was no skin off my nose. I had an advantage. I knew the plan worked, the organization was rock-solid, and the success stories were phenomenal. I still liked the person who refused to join me, but it was their loss, not mine.

I love to find people who bring a strong work ethic, commitment, and structure to the task at hand. This is who I want on my team—those who have a standard of excellence and expectation and are not going to settle for second best.

When you find men and women who have a passion for life and are determined to play at the highest level, ask them to join you. I believe there are still millions who are searching for a better life and have the ambition and desire to excel.

In our politically and socially correct world, many have

tried to label ambition as a bad thing. They constantly criticize and put down big business, yet every major corporation was birthed by someone with a dream and the ambition to make it a success.

It is hard for me to understand those who want no ceiling placed on their own progress but try to set limits on how big a company can grow. It doesn't make sense.

As the heroic general George S. Patton stated, "I do not fear failure. I only fear the 'slowing up' of the engine inside of me which is pounding, saying, 'Keep going, someone must be on top, why not you?' "

No Room for Error

I am a big fan of Coach Mike Krzyzewski of the Duke Blue Devils. His standard of excellence involves every aspect of his outstanding basketball program.

Coach K demands perfection. Say, for example, that you are only a ball boy who is there to wipe the sweat off the floor when a player goes down in practice. If you don't quickly run over and wipe the floor as fast as you can, you'll soon be replaced. Why? Because the team is allowed to practice only two hours a day. Every minute counts, and they're waiting to run the next play. If the ball boy is lazy or doesn't do a good job, a player could get injured.

Coach K asks each member of the program to give 100 percent effort all the time. This includes everyone—the trainers, the ones handing out towels and Gatorade, and those in public relations. They are all part of the team, and excellence is demanded.

A Determined Decision

Potential is overrated—it is an attribute every person possesses, but not all use it. Far more valuable is determination. It is what leads to uncommon accomplishment.

George Allen, the former coach of the Washington Redskins, made this observation: "People of mediocre ability sometimes achieve outstanding success because they don't know when to quit. Most men succeed because they are determined to."

You can have the loftiest vision in the world, but until you marry effort with self-discipline and resolve, you'll be whistling in the wind.

Ultimate achievement isn't based only on talent. You don't have to be tall enough to slam-dunk a basketball. It's not necessary to run a 4:40 forty-yard dash. You don't have to be able to hit a baseball five hundred feet. Complaining that you lack what others possess is just one more excuse for standing on the sidelines of life. You *do* have talent! You *do* have skills!

When you find a proven opportunity with a duplicable plan, it doesn't take genius or extraordinary skill—all that is required is a decision.

Are you ready to make yours?

5

THERE'S NO SUCH THING AS FAILURE

Failure should be our teacher, not our undertaker. Failure is delay, not defeat. It is a temporary detour, not a dead end.

—Denis Waitley

When I was young, I thought success was based on making the fewest mistakes possible. Was I ever wrong! Before I ventured out on my own, I was afraid to fail—even though I did.

When it came to being a productive member of society, however, I brought nothing to the table. In truth, I was part of the problem and not even close to be being part of the solution. Mine was a life of quiet desperation—I was existing, just going through the motions but not really living. I didn't know I was miserable or that I was wasting my life. I wasn't even unhappy, just stagnant and lost in my own small world.

My entire future had *failure* written all over it. I didn't know what I believed—because in the busyness of each day, I had never stopped long enough to even think about such things.

What's the Lesson?

Once I started rubbing shoulders with achievers and learning the principles of champions, I was amazed to find out that real winners are the ones who make the *most* mistakes but they don't let it bother them. They learn from each mistake and rarely make the same mistake twice. They refuse to allow their reversals to affect their confidence or self-image.

I also learned that such a person gains invaluable insight from a setback—plus, it significantly speeds up the growth process.

When my big transition came, I was now associating with people who knew who they were, where they were headed, and were making it happen. They weren't bellyaching about gas prices, the cost of a gallon of milk, the weather forecast, or life's circumstances. These men and women combined a positive mental attitude with hard work and the results were amazing.

When things take a wrong turn, a real leader will start questioning, "What can I learn from this? How can it help my future?"

When you believe success is the result of perfection, you become cautious and calculating. You are constantly looking over your shoulder and filled with anxiety. Every move you make is controlled and organized—so much so that you can't be the real you.

For some, no matter how hard they try, it seems like their life is slowly caving in. There is always confusion and they are continually taking two steps forward and three steps back. It's a sad way to exist.

In order to achieve the success I believed I deserved, I had to make some drastic changes. Sure, there would be failures, but I was determined to never quit, and bounce right back up if I ever fell. As the famous artist Pablo Picasso expressed, "Every act of creation is first of all an act of destruction. One must first break down the barriers of present limitations and destructive thoughts and destroy old habits that strangle our creative efforts. Then and only then can our creative genius be explored."

It was certainly true for me. I was not seeking perfection, but rather to work hard and work smart.

The Menu of Life

I learned firsthand from motocross racing: it's the crashes that make you strong and resilient. Never get out there on a dirt bike unless you are prepared to experience some serious bumps and bruises.

It was National Amateur Day at the 1975 AMA Motocross series at Lake Sugar Tree Motorsport Park in Axton, Virginia. I was trying to qualify for the 125 C class race. On a left-handed sweeper, my bike locked and the back end came around. I stuck my foot out to catch my balance, and it all but ended my baseball career. My knee was seriously hurt, yet before long I was back on my bike—and racing at an even higher level.

Injuries are a part of all sports, but in motocross they can be more severe. However, the risk is part of the thrill you feel when you are at the starting line, waiting for the gate to drop. It's a real adrenaline rush.

The underlying lesson, however, is that we learn from our mistakes and failures.

Something to Brag About

When I was in high school, I joined the wrestling squad. I wasn't the best on the team. Far from it. In fact, I lost to nearly every opponent I faced. But there was one saving grace—I was never pinned in a match—not once. So instead of getting uptight over my losses, I took pride in the fact that nobody could pin my shoulders to the mat. This was what gave me the gumption to continue.

Stop worrying about your losses. Flops and failures are part of the menu of life. Sadly, far too many return to the buffet for a second helping!

Learn to look at it in this light: you're not failing, you are just rehearsing. Charles F. Kettering, who held patents for everything from electric ignitions to diesel engines, observed, "An inventor fails 999 times, and if he succeeds once, he's in. He treats his failures simply as practice shots."

You're at Bat!

Always pay close attention to the advice of a winner. They have earned the right to speak.

Let's say you are a rookie baseball player who has just been brought up to the major leagues, and you are about to bat against Roger Clemens in his prime. Seated on the bench next to you is a Hall of Famer who tells you, "Roger is a great pitcher but he's very predictable. He's going to set you up with a high and inside fastball. Strike one. Then he will throw the next one down low at your knees. Strike two. Then, just when you think he's going to throw a waste pitch, here comes a wicked curveball down and out that he wants you to take a swing at. Don't fall for this. It's going to look like a ninety-mile-an-hour fastball, but at the last minute it is going to break low and away. If you swing, all you are going to do is hit a dribbler to second base or shortstop. It is going to be an out."

You have two choices. You can either take the advice of a seasoned pro, or you can brag, "I hit .340 in the minor leagues, and Clemens is getting old. I can hit anybody."

Roger is likely to be the winner either way. If you don't take the advice, you're dead meat. If you do take the counsel offered, you will learn.

As a rookie independent business owner, or a seasoned business owner looking for new ways to grow, you'll need to seek out other small business owners who have had great success in building and growing their own businesses. You need to seek out good mentors, and you need to pay attention to what they are telling you about being success-ful. Other great sources of help are business books by small business owners who have actually done the work, not just talked about it. You can either believe your mentors and other successful business owners or doubt their wisdom, but eventually you are going to find out they are right. The men and women who grow at the pace they set for themselves listen closely to those who have gone before them. They absorb the words of a person who wants them to succeed and has a vested interest in their success. They trust the advice given and duplicate the pattern.

They Proved the Critics Wrong

If there were an Encyclopedia of Errors, the list of those included would be miles long—from Napoleon to Thomas Jefferson, and plenty of notable individuals today.

When you start looking for those who failed, you will find them everywhere. But there are countless people who will prove you wrong:

- Albert Einstein was unable to speak until he was four years old and didn't read until he was seven. His teacher described him as "mentally slow, unsociable and adrift forever in his foolish dreams."
- A sports expert once said of Vince Lombardi: "He possesses minimal football knowledge. Lacks motivation."
- Beethoven preferred playing his own compositions instead of improving his violin technique. His teacher called him hopeless as a composer.
- R. H. Macy failed seven times before his department store in New York caught on with the public.
- The great baseball player Babe Ruth hit 714 home runs—but he also struck out 1,330 times.
- Leo Tolstoy, author of *War and Peace*, flunked out of college. He was once described as "both unable and unwilling to learn."
- Fred Astaire took his first Hollywood screen test. The memo from MGM's casting director read, "Can't act. Slightly bald. Can dance a little."
- Winston Churchill was a poor student. But after a lifetime of defeats and setbacks he rose to become prime minister of England at the age of sixty-six.

- John Grisham's first novel was rejected by sixteen agents and twelve publishing houses. Today he is lauded as one of the best fiction writers of the twenty-first century. Over 250 million copies of his books have been sold worldwide.

Never allow handicaps, criticism, setbacks, or rejections to become easy excuses for failure. If these people can succeed, so can you.

Build a Bridge

One of the advantages of having a business of your own is that when there is a slump in growth you can start figuring out how to inject some momentum and keep the enterprise operating. Gone is the mentality that says, *I'll let somebody else solve the crisis.* Or, *It's not up to me. It is the corporation's problem.*

If you are unwilling to discard "job" thinking, you are going to be one frustrated individual. Start taking your role as a business owner or head of your own organization seriously and turn roadblocks into bridges. If the problem is financial, don't view it as an expense, rather as an investment in your future.

Norman Vincent Peale was once approached by a young man who wanted to start his own business but lamented that he had no money. I love Peale's response: "Empty pockets never held anyone back. Only empty heads and empty hearts can do that."

Some of the greatest opportunities in the world require very little money to get started. It was true for me—and for millions of others.

Here's something else I discovered: you can't keep a quitter from quitting, and you can never keep a winner from winning. This was why I decided to build my business with winners.

Don't Major in Minors

One of the best stress relievers I practice is not to worry about trivial events. If what I am going through won't matter five or ten years down the road, why should I develop ulcers over it today? Why become anxious and lose sleep when the issue is not life-threatening?

It wouldn't hurt to live by the words of author Robert Eliot: "Rule #1: Don't sweat the small stuff. Rule #2: It's all small stuff."

You may reach the point where you think your situation is insurmountable. Sorry to break the news, but almost nobody else really cares. Out of the billions of people on the planet, you're probably the only one concerned. The president is not meeting with his Cabinet to discuss it, and Billy Graham doesn't have it on his prayer list!

Since you are going to make most of life's choices on your own, take it from one who knows: never make a major decision regarding finances or your family when you are emotional, tired, or when it's late at night. Wait until the sun is shining and take a fresh look at the problem in the light of day.

Treat a minor setback for what it is—a small matter in the scheme of things. It's been said that we stumble over pebbles, not over mountains.

As singer Dolly Parton said, "If you want the rainbow, you've got to put up with the rain."

Get Moving!

I heard about a young Little League pitcher who knew he was in trouble when the coach walked up to him and said, "Son, I think I better have someone relieve you."

"But," the pitcher pleaded, "I struck this guy out the last time."

"I know," replied the coach, "but this is the same inning!"

If you maintain the right attitude, the more you fail, the faster you will succeed. And when you bungle big-time, don't sit in a corner and have a pity party. Start taking action immediately, even though you may have to force yourself to get moving.

Success is based on failure and remaining enthusiastic no matter what.

I learned how to expect and project—and how a dream that is linked with activity will unveil a whole new world.

When you finally get your attitude and thought process fine-tuned and adjusted, it becomes easy. Here's the conclusion I have come to: I would rather have a crumb of information from the table of a super-successful person than a feast from a failure.

In the books I read, one of the constant themes in most of them was the power of expectation. But simply envisioning a positive outcome was only part of the answer. I had to stand on my feet and *do* something about it!

Paul the Apostle, who wrote nearly one-half of the New Testament, gave some tremendous advice to the Philippians when he said, "Whatever is true, whatever is noble, whatever is right, whatever is pure, whatever is lovely, whatever is admirable—if anything is excellent or praiseworthy—think about such things."

However, his very next words hold the secret to real success: "Whatever you have learned or received or heard from me, or seen in me—put it into practice."

As the Nike slogan says, "Just do it!"

Never worry or be nervous about saying the wrong thing; just worry about saying *something!*

The person who lives in constant fear of making mistakes rarely succeeds. Failure is the way we learn. Making the most of our mistakes is how we grow! Remember, thoughts become things! They turn into reality.

Reload

Being good-looking, funny, smart, athletic, or perfect are not prerequisites for becoming an achiever. In fact, you don't have to be anything but the best you can be.

Your "best" will not always come naturally. It's the result of dusting yourself off when you are knocked down and reloading when you misfire. Get tough on yourself. Go through the pressure and persevere—and eventually a lump of coal becomes a brilliant diamond of value.

As Dale Carnegie, author of *How to Win Friends and Influence People*, wrote: "Don't be afraid to give your best to what seemingly are small jobs. Every time you conquer one it makes you that much stronger. If you do the little jobs well, the big ones will tend to take care of themselves."

Even though I was far from a polished person, and had so much improving to do, I was willing to take risks that others wouldn't so I could enjoy rewards others couldn't even fathom.

The Magic Formula

It has been said that the guy who never learns from his mistakes will wind up taking orders from one who does!

It's okay, even human, to make bad decisions. Just try not to keep making the same ones over and over again. You will find that the foundation of success is built on a series of failures you don't keep repeating.

Here's the magic formula: you try, you fail, you adjust. Tomorrow you do the same thing: try, fail, and adjust.

However, if you fail to correct a mistake—you've just committed another one!

As humorist Josh Billings once remarked, "It ain't no disgrace for a man to fall, but to lie there and grunt is."

The daughter of noted writer Ralph Waldo Emerson was attending boarding school. In one of the letters she wrote to her family, she shared how concerned she was about a mistake she had made that was bothering her greatly. She couldn't get it out of her mind.

There is a wonderful truth in the response Emerson wrote to his daughter: "Finish every day and be done with it. You have done what you could. Some blunders and absurdities no doubt crept in. But get rid of them and forget them as soon as you can. Tomorrow is a new day, and you should never encumber its potentialities and invitations with the dread of the past. You should not waste a moment on the rottenness of yesterday."

Perhaps there is an event in your life to which you can apply these words.

Take Responsibility

When you do make an error, quickly accept the blame. Never pass the buck or make a million phony excuses. The world respects the man or woman who owns up to their foul-ups and has the courage to stand and admit, "I did it. This was my fault, but I won't let it happen again."

As one friend said, "If you mess up, 'fess up!"

If you are sincere, and your apology is spoken from the heart, others will honor your integrity. It clears the air and allows you to move on.

Learn to recognize the truth that failure is an *event*—and avoid thinking it is a person. It is simply something that happened and should never be tied to the reputation or character of an individual.

"Temporary Income"

For most of my young years, I floated through life finding excuses for the circumstances in which I found myself. It wasn't until I reached rock bottom that I had to look myself in the mirror and say, "Larry, you got yourself into this mess—and now it's time to get yourself out!"

The reason I talk about broke people is because I am an authority on the topic—that was me. Unfortunately, broke people perpetuate "broke-ness." I know how they think, how they operate, and why they are in such a desperate condition.

A financial planner told me recently that almost everybody is broke—some are broke at a higher level.

In today's economy, more and more jobs are falling into the category of "temporary income." At the slightest sign of a downturn, your employer can pull the rug out from under you without blinking an eye.

If you are out of work for ninety days and the bank is threatening to foreclose on your house, you're in trouble—whether it's a $90,000 home or a $900,000 mansion.

I was where I was because of my thoughts and actions—or lack of them. So, since I dug my own hole, I decided to change what was going on in my mind and in my behavior.

A major reason people fail to become achievers is because they do not accept personal responsibility for where they are in life. They can offer a dozen excuses, but they all ring hollow until they confess, "It's me! I'm at fault. So I've got to straighten myself out!"

Thankfully, I learned principles and truths that allowed me to break free from the crushing burden I was carrying. With God's help, I was able to catch a glimpse of my future and seize it!

Losing Produces Champions

I firmly believe that no matter what happens, some good can come out of everything.

Perhaps you've noticed that when an athletic team wins game after game, the players may become so cocky and overconfident they are uncoachable. This is why a great basketball coach doesn't mind an embarrassing loss in the middle of an otherwise perfect season.

Now he has the chance to take control of his players,

bring them back down to earth, and get busy with some serious practice time. As a result, the team becomes united and much stronger.

Inch by Inch

If you want to reverse a disappointment, it's okay to have a big vision, but take the time to write out a plan that will get you there and take it inch by inch. It's paying attention to small stuff along the way that will move you to your ultimate target.

This is what Thomas Edison did. He was asked about all the failures he experienced while he was in the process of inventing the lightbulb. He stated, "I haven't failed; I've just found ten thousand ways that didn't work."

Bounce Back

I have to confess, it bugs me to be around people who constantly talk about topics that don't really matter. It gets a little boring when the only conversation involves how a politician in government is failing—or giving all the intimate details of an uncle's operation, someone I don't even know!

Winners delight in talking about their future—their goals, dreams, and opportunities.

I've been accused of being a fanatic when it comes to success. I'm guilty as charged, and I take that as a compliment. Yes, I am fanatical when it comes to overcoming the odds, bouncing back from defeat, and being the person God intends for me to be.

King Solomon, the wisest man who ever lived, wrote,

"Though the righteous fall seven times, they rise again, but the wicked stumble when calamity strikes."

Who are the mentors you are going to listen to? Those who fall but are too bruised to stand back up? The critics? The excuse makers? The dream stealers?

Success is within the ability of every person—and so is failure. It's up to you to decide how you want to live.

6

THE KEY TO AN "OTHERS" MENTALITY

The entire population of the universe, with one trifling exception, is composed of others.
—John Andrew Holmes

In the days when I was pushing a twenty-one-inch Murray lawn mower from house to house, I ran into people who fell into three different categories. I have heard them called "lawn mower people."

I've met them all my life—from the time I played baseball and raced motocross to this very moment.

Do any of these three categories sound familiar?

Lawn Mower Person #1—The Complainer

A neighbor looks across the street at your lawn and sees that it's overgrown. The grass is supposed to be no more than four or five inches high, and yours sprouted much higher. This disgruntled man says to himself, "That's bringing down the image of our whole street."

He won't approach you, but he doesn't hesitate to call the fellow next door and complain: "Can you believe those people? What a mess their yard is! If it doesn't get mowed it will lower our property values."

This guy might even call a city or county government office, knowing there are ordinances regulating how high the grass has to be before they send out a notice. They may even come with a mower—and charge the resident.

Lacking the backbone to talk with you face-to-face, he would rather gripe to anyone who will listen, spreading rumors because your yard doesn't meet his standards.

For all he knows, you could have been in the hospital and had back surgery. He doesn't know the real reason why the grass isn't mowed. His complaints are based only on what he sees.

Lawn Mower Person #2—The Confronter

This is the individual who looks at the condition of your yard and immediately rings your doorbell. He then looks you in the eye and says, "Your grass is too tall, and I think you need to do something about it."

You may have a valid reason why the weeds are growing out of control, but this neighbor couldn't care less. The confronter just wants you to get that yard mowed—now!

At least he had the gumption to tell you up close and personal without spreading poison behind your back. The confronter has confronted you—and that's as far as it goes.

Lawn Mower Person #3—The Helper

This is the neighbor who casually walks over and, after a friendly greeting, says, "I see your grass is overgrown. Is there anything I can do to help?"

The reason might be as simple as the fact you ran out of gas or your mower is broken. You thank him for stopping by and explain, "I tried to get it started and couldn't—then it rained for a few days. That grass has really grown like crazy."

The excuse doesn't bother this neighbor, who asks, "Have you checked the spark plug?"

"Never thought of that, but I don't have another one," you reply.

Without batting an eye, he tells you, "Give me a second. I think I have a spare in my garage."

In a few minutes, you pull on the engine cord and zooooom—it's working again. You mow your lawn, and all is right in the neighborhood.

If Only They Had Told Me

In my world today, I still meet these three categories of people, but there's only one type I enjoy spending my time with—those who have an "others" mentality.

At one point, I was controlled by the whims and wishes of those who lorded over me. I didn't know how to boldly stand on my own two feet and be assertive. Instead, I was temperamental and could fly off the handle at a moment's notice. But that wasn't getting me anywhere.

I wish someone had told me while I was in junior high or high school what it took me years to learn. I'm not placing blame anywhere; that's just the way it was. I was even a Boy Scout, but I don't remember them explaining what really mattered in life—they just helped me earn merit badges.

Inside of me, waiting to be awakened, were unlimited, God-given abilities that I had never thought of or exercised. They were dormant.

Thankfully, things changed. I found myself around a group of people who were not shy with their encouragement. One person after another was telling me: "You can be more than you are, do more than you do, and achieve more than you have. Hang in there!"

Slowly but surely, their words began to sink into my soul and spirit. It took time, but I finally realized that I no longer had to live a humdrum life of mediocrity. Being "average" could be a thing of the past.

Peeling the Onion

Today, I thank God for those who cared enough to surround me with hope, faith, belief, expectation, and optimism. They became my answer.

It should come as no surprise that their consistent love and support rang a bell in my spirit. The day came when I had a talk with myself and concluded, *If these people can take the time to pour their best into me, I have an obligation to do the same for others.*

As I read, listened, and attended conventions and business events, I was like an onion being peeled away layer after layer until I saw the truth within myself.

When I had a "taking" mentality I was continually running on empty. It was only when I had a change of heart and turned my eyes toward others that I grew as a person.

It really wasn't that difficult. In my new business, I saw people serving me, and I began to serve others. My confusion began to dissipate, and I started seeing as never before. Finally, I was no longer influenced by those who were still fumbling in the fog.

Once I became strong, I was able to provide strength for others—until the cobwebs were also blown from *their* minds.

I Was Mesmerized

I still smile when I remember the night someone presented a business opportunity to me for the first time. I was fascinated by how the fellow could write with a blue marker on a shiny whiteboard, wipe it off, and leave no chalk residue!

I'd never seen that before and was mesmerized. I thought there must be some electronics involved somewhere.

When it was my turn to show what I had learned, I bumbled through it in ten minutes and didn't have a clue what I was doing. I'm glad there was no video camera recording my presentation, or I'd be embarrassed to this day.

However, a friend whom I had invited to join me caught the same vision I had. Now, many years later, the organization he developed has produced tremendous financial security for both his family and mine.

It wasn't a bad night!

Today, I am continually asked, "Larry, is it still possible to have an unlimited income?"

I can guarantee you it is, and there are people who will guide, mentor, and encourage you along the way. They can't force you to be successful, but if you stay the course and follow the proven business principles I've shared in this book and your mentors have shared as sources of their success, you will build a strong team, and over time you'll find that you can't stop the growth.

What a trip!

No Backstabbing

In October 1980, two months after birthing this new enterprise, I was invited to attend a business rally in Richmond, Virginia. It was quite an eye-opener! I'd never seen anything like it. The inspiring speakers spoke of having a purpose, being free, and changing lives. There was no dog-eat-dog, backstabbing, success-at-any-cost language.

I am proud to tell you that the people I have associated with from the very beginning are men and women of honor, character, and integrity. They were not perfect—and there's nothing wrong with trying to be—but the standards and values they were striving for raised the bar for me.

Once I caught the vision that I could be changed, I also saw how those around me could be, too. It wasn't all about me. I began believing in others.

Let me offer this word of advice: when you start a business of your own that involves an organization and other team members, it's only normal to wonder if you'll make it. You may even be tempted to throw in the towel before the first round of the fight is over.

Remembering my own start, I lost the right to quit the moment I told the first person in my business, "I'll help you."

That was the pledge I made—and I had to stick by my word. How could I walk away from a promise?

You're Not Alone

The responsibility of any leader is to set an example—in attitude, vision, self-discipline, character, enthusiasm, confidence, composure, and a commitment to excellence.

Taking on a leadership role should include being so strong that the weakest person can lean on you until they are able to support themselves. To be truly successful, however, you must find a cause bigger than yourself and a reason greater than recognition or money.

I was in business *for* myself, but quickly learned I was not in business *by* myself.

When I use the words "my business," I am really referring to "the *people* in my business."

I am so grateful I am working with men, women, and entire families who are now my friends. They are the dearest people in the world to Pam and me. They aren't out there blindly climbing the face of a mountain alone. I am helping them with every step.

A lot of baggage in my life was discarded when I began to see people as friends—not as enemies or competitors—and awoke to the fact that we are more alike than we are different.

What I am sharing is true for every type of enterprise I can think of—whether a mom-and-pop dry cleaner, an Internet shopping site, or a fast food franchise. If you fail to put the customer first, your business may soon be ranked last.

I chuckled when I heard about a grocery clerk who got tired of his job and decided to quit and become a policeman. A few days later, a friend asked him, "How do you like your new line of work?"

The fellow paused for a moment and replied, "The pay and the hours aren't too good, but at least the customer is always wrong!"

One in a Million!

Make sure your priorities are right.

The owner of a local dry cleaner whose business was booming was asked, "What's the key to your success?"

He didn't hesitate with his answer: "Each day, I act as if we are on the verge of losing every customer."

This attitude must apply to enterprises small or large. For example, an executive at IBM was questioned, "If your failure rate is one in a million, what do you tell that one customer?"

He thought for a moment and said, "We treat every customer as if he or she is one in a million!"

That's not just the *right* attitude—it is the *only* attitude worth putting into practice.

When Marshall Field was walking through his original department store in Chicago, he heard a clerk heatedly arguing with a customer. Immediately, he walked over and asked the employee, "What are you doing?"

The clerk answered, "I'm settling a complaint."

Field quickly replied, "No, you're not. Give the lady what she wants."

It's no wonder that the Marshall Field stores became such a giant success.

Those you are serving must never be seen as an interruption in your work—they are the very reason your enterprise exists. Also, remember that you aren't doing them a special favor when you serve them. Just the opposite: they are blessing you by requesting your service or product.

If someone were to ask, "Who is the most important person in your business?" how would you respond? I hope you already know the answer: the customer. Without that individual, your operation wouldn't be in existence.

Ray Kroc, who founded McDonald's, came to this conclusion: "A well-run restaurant is like a winning baseball team. It makes the most of every crew member's talents and takes advantage of every split-second opportunity to speed up service." Everything is directed toward pleasing the person who places the order. He added, "If you work just for money, you'll never make it, but if you love what you're doing and you always put the customer first, success will be yours."

When you grow an organization based on harmony and a genuine love for people, your productivity will soar through the roof.

Words Worth Remembering

I don't know who wrote "The Most Important Words in the World," but they are certainly worth remembering:

- The six most important words: "I admit I made a mistake."
- The five most important words: "You did a good job."
- The four most important words: "What is *your* opinion?"
- The three most important words: "If you please..."
- The two most important words: "Thank you."
- The most important word: "We."
- The least important word: "I."

Make sure you have things in the right perspective.
The principle of "we" applies across the board—whether

you are recruiting volunteers to clean a mile of a highway or running a billion-dollar corporation. There will never be success unless people check their egos at the door. There won't be much progress if you have a bunch of superstars insisting, "You've got to do it my way."

Any basketball coach will tell you that it's not the five best players who win championships, it is the five who play the best together.

It reminds me of the confident mouse who said to the elephant as they were walking across a bridge: "Together, we're shaking this thing!"

It Takes More Than One

A troop of Boy Scouts gathered for their annual hike in the woods. Taking off at sunrise, they began a fifteen-mile trek through a beautiful valley. About halfway on their walk they came across an abandoned section of railroad track.

Each of the boys tried to walk the narrow rails, but after only a few unsteady steps, each boy would lose his balance and fall off.

Two of the scouts, after watching their friends fall, offered a bet to the rest of the troop. They bragged, "I bet we can walk the entire length of the railroad track without losing our footing, even once."

"No way," the others said.

Ready to make good on their bet, the two jumped on opposite rails and simply reached out and held hands to balance each other. They steadily walked the entire section of track with no difficulty.

Who Have You Helped?

You will see this exact same principle at work as you build your business.

When you pull out the records at the end of the month, the bottom line called "profit" lets you know how productive you are as the owner.

Never think you made this happen all by yourself. Stop for a moment and realize it's all about people—people move products; products don't move people. When you constantly support and cheer on the individuals involved, you will inevitably increase volume or see far greater response to the services you offer.

In the words of a proverb, "Help your brother's boat across, and your own will reach the shore."

Another old adage is still true: if you help enough people get what they want, you automatically get what you want.

But here's the catch. You can't force someone into being served—you have to find a willing participant. Any type of coercion will ultimately fail. But if you reach out with sincerity in your heart, you will find plenty who are ready to join your cause.

I can assure you from my own experience that it's much easier to work with those who truly want what you have to offer. I love mentoring men and women on the principles of success, but I am quick to let them know that it can't be handed to them on a silver platter.

As you are building a team and growing your independent business organization, you will find that people generally fall into three categories: (1) quitters, (2) incubators, and (3) performers.

Listen closely to what a person says and watch what they do. If their words are not backed up by their actions, take them out of the active "building-business" profile and put them in the "social club incubator."

They may be kidding themselves, but if you allow them to fool you, two have failed. As I like to say, "My eleventh commandment is 'Thou shalt not fooleth thyself.' "

The Word Will Spread

If you decide to become a business owner, you'd better start thinking like one.

Let me give this example: if you are unhappy with your food at a restaurant, the waiter or waitress may or may not make it right. However, if you get the attention of the owner, he or she will bend over backward to make sure you are pleased. There's a huge investment at stake.

It's been proven that every satisfied customer is likely to tell three friends about your business. This is what you want. Word of mouth is the best free advertising in the world. On the other hand, every unhappy customer will gripe to at least ten people. I suppose it's because angry people let off more steam,

Make sure the odds stay in your favor.

Here is what those in the hospitality business have discovered over the years. Guest recognition is better than guest rewards. This is why so many country clubs and first-class hotel chains train their employees to remember the names of their guests. You beat the competition by giving people personal attention, sincerity, and a "no request is too small" attitude.

Walk into any Ritz-Carlton, and after an encounter with a

team member you will likely hear the phrase, "My pleasure."
That phrase can work everywhere.

Joining Forces

As I revisit my past, I am reminded that I had to lay the
groundwork for my business to become the giant enterprise that it is. During those years, however, I worked hard,
stayed focused, developed a positive work ethic, sowed
seed, served, and encouraged to the best of my God-given
ability.

The growth of our organization has skyrocketed because
of our bond of unity. None of this is the result of any one
person's ability, ego, or pride. It is because men and women
with amazing individual talents joined forces to say:

- "We want to be involved in what truly matters."
- "We want to spread the good news of free enterprise."
- "We want to lift people and help them do something
  special with their lives."
- "We want to travel with friends, to experience the
  world and share memories."
- "We want to keep our country free."

These are your friends and neighbors who were tired of
the status quo and were ready for so much more. Sure, it
would take a little extra energy and greater commitment—
but look at the benefits.

The reason I had the faith to envision such a huge number
of people in our organization wasn't simply based on hope
and expectation. Rather, my faith was built on the track record
we had established by people helping people. We have grown

one handshake at a time. I never say, "This is how many we have," rather, "This is how many we have helped."

I believe the words of author Alan Loy McGinnis: "There is no more noble occupation in the world than to assist another human being—to help someone succeed."

Give It Away

I laughed out loud when a friend told me, "It's all relative. Because when you start making money, all the relatives come out of the woodwork."

When I became in a position to help certain people, I didn't give them a loan—because of the guilt they might have felt if they couldn't pay me back. If I did decide to help, I was thrilled to say, "This is a gift; yours to keep."

Author Paul Flemming sums it up this way: "Happiness is the cheapest thing in the world when we buy it for someone else."

I only bring this topic up purely to show what we have been blessed to do for others, and not for a pat on the back. Far from it. I want it to be an example that communicates: *Look at what you can do to help your fellow man. This is what your future is going to be like.*

Albert Schweitzer, the noted humanitarian, made this observation: "I don't know what your destiny will be, but one thing I do know. The only ones among you who will be truly happy are those who will have sought and found how to serve." And he added, "Life becomes harder for us when we live for others, but it also becomes richer and happier."

I slept through plenty of high school classes, but when I woke up, I never saw those words written on anybody's paper.

Fifty-Six Fearless Men

Individually, you are limited and can accomplish only so much. But when we band together, look out world! To paraphrase the Good Book: "One can chase a thousand, but two can put ten thousand to flight."

This is proof that you can slay giants.

Think back a couple of centuries when fifty-six men signed the Declaration of Independence on July 4, 1776. They were basically a mix of farmers and merchants with no military experience, and at that time there was no organized defense in the Colonies.

All they shared was an ideal—a goal that was much greater than any of them could accomplish alone. The Founding Fathers were convinced they could no longer exist under the restrictions and penalties ordered by the government of the British empire thousands of miles across the sea. Those fifty-six brave men signed the document with these words: "For the support of this declaration, with firm reliance on the protection of the divine providence, we mutually pledge to each other our lives, our fortunes, and our sacred honor."

There were a litany of reasons they didn't want to be subjected to England's rule any longer—and it had very little to do with money or business.

The British thought they could squash the rebellion because of their well-trained army and their heralded naval power. But the Revolutionary War wasn't based on military tactics. Volunteer militias rose up in America and fought with such bravery that the British were humiliated and finally defeated in 1783.

How was this possible? Because ordinary people joined

forces with a common cause, an ideal—that man should live with liberty.

Nine of those original fifty-six men died in the battles of the revolution and never tasted the fruits of independence. They sacrificed their lives, their "sacred honor," so that you and I could be free.

Reaching Out to You

You may have been raised in a home where there was zero encouragement and practically no praise. Some have grown up bombarded with both verbal and nonverbal pessimism that engraves the message *You'll never make it. You don't have what it takes.*

If this reflects your upbringing, right now, press the Delete button on your inner computer. Erase the bad data, take a deep breath, and start recording again.

Link your life with people who not only have a vision for *their* future, but also yours! When they reach out with their hearts, accept their love. When they show you a better path, follow their leadership. When they offer to mentor you, listen closely. Then step out with the belief and confidence that you are a new *you*!

When you hang around those who have a burning passion for success and are on fire, eventually your wet blanket will dry out. Before long, your enthusiasm will ignite others to carry the torch.

Starving for Encouragement

In Aubrey Daniels's insightful book, *Bringing Out the Best in People*, he tells what steps to take when you are given the opportunity to manage a new department or group of people where the morale is low.

He recommends finding one individual who stands out above the crowd, then call a meeting and start bragging on that person. Those who have been dragging their heels, mumbling and grumbling, will start looking for a project they can excel in so that you will shine the spotlight on them, too.

People are starving for words of encouragement. This is why you must love and serve those who are on your team— and even those who are not.

Edgar Watson Howe, a noted journalist, offers this advice: "When a friend is in trouble, don't annoy him by asking if there is anything you can do. Think up something appropriate and do it."

Would She Live?

It doesn't need to be a life-or-death situation in order to ask, "What am I willing to give?"

I heard the story of a ten-year-old boy named Jimmy, who was devoted to his little sister, age six. She was his best friend. You can imagine his panic when she fell off her bicycle and severed a large artery in her leg. The bleeding was profuse, and by the time the family rushed her to a doctor, the youngster was failing fast.

This happened at a time before blood transfusions were common practice.

The doctor managed to put a clamp on the cut ends of the artery, but the girl was dying. He turned to Jimmy, and asked, "Will you give your blood to help save your sister's life?"

Jimmy blinked for a moment, swallowed hard, and

bravely nodded his head. So the doctor laid him on a table and began taking blood from one of his veins—and infusing it directly into his sister.

The next thirty minutes were critical, as the physician and family anxiously watched and prayed over the little girl.

When the crisis was over and she sat up, the doctor looked over and saw Jimmy—still stretched out on the table, trembling.

"Jimmy, what on earth is the matter?" he asked.

Through his clenched teeth, Jimmy replied, "W-w-when do I die?"

Not fully understanding, this devoted brother was willing to give his all!

You Can Be the Answer

On our journey, Pam and I have learned how to make money, but in the process we have discovered something far more valuable—how to make a lasting difference in the lives of others.

We were thrown a lifeline, and now we have become "lifeline throwers." We fully understand that "to whom much is given, from him much will be required."

Never be embarrassed to ask enough questions to determine how you can help the most. Perhaps your advice is directed toward a person's attitude, work habits, or marriage. You may not have all the solutions, but just the fact you are interested and willing to help may be the answer they need. What a gift you are. A friend to talk with—a shoulder to cry on—an encourager who can lift their spirits and cause them to smile again.

Start Serving

If I can inspire just one twenty-year-old out of the nightclubs and bars or away from his computer games and other time wasters, what I am doing will be worth the effort.

When a person is broke or lonely, he often doesn't know any other way to live. But you and I can show them how. Very few are strong enough to empower someone else to be more than they can be, but I believe you have that capacity.

We have all heard of the famous Mayo Clinic in Rochester, Minnesota. It was founded by Dr. Charles Mayo and his brother, William.

Once, "Dr. Charlie," as he was known, was host to an Englishman who stayed as a guest in his home. Just before retiring for the night, the visitor placed his shoes outside the bedroom door, expecting a servant to give them a shine.

The next morning, the shoes were perfectly polished— by Dr. Charles Mayo himself.

What a demonstration of humility. This is what it means to serve!

Pass It On

If you are lost and struggling to get from one destination to another, you'd better avoid giving anyone else instructions. You can't teach what you don't know, and you can't give what you don't have. Only those with food can help people who are hungry.

Pam and I are the first to admit we don't know every-thing, but we have learned some valuable lessons along the way, and we are more than thrilled to pass them on to whoever will listen. Nothing will give us greater joy than to see you do more than you ever dreamed and impact more lives than we have already touched.

Bury every excuse you've given for staying where you are and closing the door to a new opportunity. Please don't let life pass you by. Just as there were wonderful individuals who reached out to me, someone will be there for you.

Perhaps Ronald Reagan said it best: "I'm convinced more than ever that man finds liberation only when he binds himself to God and commits himself to his fellow man."

Step into the circle of life and discover what an "others" mentality is all about.

7

Find Your Personal Why

Many men go fishing all of their lives without knowing it is not fish they are after.
—Henry David Thoreau

How you build a business is only part of the equation; you have to determine the reason behind your actions. I firmly believe your personal *why* is an essential ingredient, and one only you can discover.

Since no two people are alike, this will vary. For many, however, it is just the satisfaction of being able to say, "I did it! I won! I succeeded!"

In the early days, one of my *why*s was to prove people wrong—especially those who felt it their duty to tell me, "You'll never make it." "You are not cut out for this." "You don't have the people skills."

Those were fighting words to me and became a daily driving force.

You see, when a winner becomes challenged, it doesn't

defeat him. Instead, it inspires him and spurs him on. So the more people laughed at me, the more determination I mustered. Their chiding was like food to a starving man.

When there is a valid reason that inspires and motivates, you'll soon realize how easy the techniques and how-tos are for giving you the ability to reach your objective. An instruction manual doesn't make the difference between whether or not you will be successful; it is the purpose you bring with you.

Knowing and fully understanding the passion behind your actions is essential—whether you are teaching a Sunday School class, directing a community health organization, selling cell phones, or building a business empire.

He Wasn't Thrilled

To have my mom and dad and Pam's parents be proud of me was something I longed for. After all, who wants their daughter to marry a guy who is going to spend the rest of his life telling drivers at the car wash to "Put it in neutral and take the brakes off"?

Even though Pam and I were engaged for five years, her dad hardly said a word to me. Putting it mildly, he wasn't overly excited about seeing his little girl spend a lifetime with a man who had no future.

My, how things have changed. Now, I like to think I'm his favorite relative!

Thankful, but Not Satisfied

As I write this, our *why*s today are not the ones we started with. They grew and changed just as we did. Yes, there were goals I set for myself when I began. But what if I had been content to celebrate a short-term achievement and announce, "That's it! I've arrived!"? It would have been the end of my journey.

I had to keep resetting my objectives again and again. Sure, I have been excited with every aspect of my adventure, but I'm not settling for less than the best. I'm thankful, but it certainly doesn't mean I am satisfied. I can still learn more, have more, and give more.

Never Again!

I have no problem with those who are motivated by a new opportunity primarily for economic reasons. In fact, I can relate to it very well.

I remember when Tara was just eleven months old. She became very sick with a 105-degree temperature, and we had to rush her to the hospital. At first the doctors thought she had meningitis, but the tests proved otherwise. It was two long weeks before her fever broke and she was better. Like so many other young couples, we had no insurance and ran up a hospital bill that was over $10,000.

When the crisis was over, I told myself, *Larry, you are never going to be in this situation again.*

It was one more of the *why*s that pushed me to drive more miles, talk to more people, and build a business that would transform the future of our family. I didn't go around complaining or making excuses about our problems—I kept them to myself. But one thing was for sure: I made a covenant with God that my life was going to change.

What Turned Me On

Let's be honest. In the beginning I decided to build a business of my own because the money sounded good. The second attention getter was that I wanted the freedom to set my own clock and have the option to do whatever I wanted. Third, I saw it as a way to earn respect—from those I loved and friends in the community.

It didn't take long, however, until those reasons seemed to fade into the background. Because the principles and truths I was learning had permeated my very soul, I began to see a large business organization as a way to touch countless lives for good—to show them a better and more fulfilling way to live. This really turned me on, and the passion has never diminished. In fact, it grows stronger year after year.

Without question, I was able to escape from the mess my life had become because of the message of faith that was being poured into me day after day, month after month. Without the power of divine inspiration I would have never made it.

Is Cash Really King?

Money is not the secret of happiness—but neither is poverty and debt. It is the *love* of riches that is the root of all evil. I've met wealthy people to whom money is their god—yet they can be among the most miserable men and women you'll ever know.

When was the last time you heard of a multimillionaire robbing a convenience store, shooting a clerk, or breaking into a bank? These are usually the acts of desperate people who love money, but have none. However, there are plenty of Wall Street executives in prison at this very moment because they cooked the books and stole millions from unsuspecting investors.

Money itself is never the problem—it's what happens when people lust after it. Riches can be a tool for either good or evil, depending on the motives of the heart.

I believe that money in the right hands can have a positive and permanent impact on our planet. It's been said that money is like manure: if you spread it around, it does a world of good; but if you pile it up, it stinks to high heaven!

It is in the giving that we discover true wealth.

Job Security?

A half century ago, if you asked a man or woman why they worked so hard, they would likely tell you, "For job security and a company pension."

Wow, how things have changed. The idea of a guaranteed career with one firm or organization is over. Job security? Forget about it. Not only have jobs been outsourced, entire companies have pulled up stakes and relocated to China or Mexico.

A friend of mine went to work for a company that had never laid anyone off in their one hundred years of existence. This was why he decided to work there. He chose it because of security.

Eleven months later they laid off fifteen hundred people, and he was one of them—educated, qualified, trained, hardworking men and women. Gone. The past didn't matter, and it wasn't personal. The accountants looked at the books, and the CEO was forced to make a difficult decision.

There are millions who sold their souls to a company and

truly believed that because of their dedication and loyalty they were indispensable. Can you imagine the sick feeling in the pits of their stomachs when they were called in to hear the news? "We're going to cut back, thin down, and restructure. And for some of you, this means we have to let you go."

You are ushered into an office, given a small severance package and a token thank-you. After a year or so, your severance and unemployment checks have dried up and you are unable to find a new job. Your home is on the verge of foreclosure. If you are fortunate enough to find work, you have to start at the bottom of the ladder for less pay and start climbing all over again.

Perhaps you didn't lose your house, but your mortgage is so high you wish you had. Maybe your car didn't get repossessed, yet every month it's a nightmare trying to make the payments.

For those in such a position, their original *why* for having a business of their own isn't hard to figure out. Yes, there will be some individuals who look at what you have to offer and say, "Well, it looks to me like it's just about money."

If they would only be honest and examine their lives. That's exactly what they do every workday, from six o'clock in the morning until six o'clock at night. They are chasing a paycheck.

The same person who constantly complains that others are too materialistic will drive a half hour to save a nickel a gallon on a fill-up. It doesn't make sense.

A Self-Fulfilling Prophecy

I firmly believe that if left alone, people can bounce back from any economic slowdown. Some of the problems we face may be the result of the mass media preaching fear and doubt in order to spike their ratings. Some of the problems may be our paying too much attention to negative people around us who look at the glass being half empty rather than half full. We have to be careful to guard against being caught up in the panic that oftentimes sweeps the masses, contributing to household spending grinding to a halt, companies downsizing, and talk about recession, depression, and worse. It can be a self-fulfilling prophecy. And one that creates fear in the hearts of people.

I chose to be an optimistic, independent business owner with a team of associates selling great products because it's the perfect enterprise for any economic climate. In boom times, people buy more of what I'm selling; in a rough job market, more individuals decide to come on board. It's a win-win situation.

When you make the decision to row your own boat on the sea of life, there will be plenty of options. For example, you have the right to either succeed or fail.

I cannot emphasize this enough. It is important that you join an organization that is built on people helping people. Find an atmosphere where there is plenty of learning and personal growth, and the team members are serving others.

Do your homework and know who you are linking up with. Will you find yourself in a positive atmosphere? Do the leaders have integrity and moral character? Do you want to follow their example and live their lifestyle?

If the lights are all green, start moving! There's plenty of room at the top.

As you progress, don't focus on recognition but on results. After all, you can't feed your family and your ego at the same time. Humility and hard work will cause your business to grow to the point where you will be serving more people than you ever dreamed.

Trading Hours for Dollars

In the early days, I was rather naive. I figured that if I was fired up and turned on by the business opportunity I saw, so would everybody else.

Far from it. I didn't know how dependent and complacent most people are. It was obvious that practically everyone could use the extra money, so I was shocked so few were willing to try. Was I the only one who was turned on by the idea of financial freedom?

As I look back, however, I realize I was no different. I spent years just like the average Joe—trading hours for dollars. And at the end of the week, after my bills were paid, the money had vanished, so I had to start all over again.

When another person is signing your check, that person decides whether you receive an increase or a bonus. As a result, my economic mind-set was that I had no control over what money I could earn, regardless of how much profit the company made from my efforts.

Ask the millions who lost their jobs in the recent financial downturn. Their income proved to be temporary, and as a result they became economically unstable.

The only real security today is in the ability to perform. If a man or woman has poor skills and a low self-image, they are relying on somebody else's security.

If you have bought into the notion that the government can take care of you from cradle to grave, it's time for you to step back from the brink of disaster. You're living in a fantasy world.

Your future may be comprised of many components, but the number one factor is *you!* Nothing can replace self-discipline and self-reliance. In the words of an old proverb, "The best place to find a helping hand is at the end of your own arm."

An opportunity is absolutely useless unless you seize it and make it yours. The wisdom of William Jennings Bryan is still worth repeating: "Destiny is not a matter of chance, it is a matter of choice; it is not a thing to be waited for, it is a thing to be achieved."

The Extra Mile

Far too many are under the false impression they can be self-employed, but an entrepreneur can't survive with job mentality. If you are concerned only with doing the minimum in order to keep your position and your paycheck, you're probably not cut out for the life we are talking about.

To be an entrepreneur you have to be able to provide more service than is expected, walk the extra mile, and work more hours than you ever imagined.

The real difference, however, is that when you are a success, the rewards are so much greater that anything the typical job can offer. Few people grasp this truth.

A Guaranteed Salary?

It was quite a day when my boss came to me all excited. "Larry, we have decided to give you a promotion from hourly pay to a guaranteed weekly salary."

Inside, I was jumping up and down. *Oh boy! This is good. I'm going to get paid no matter what.*

He added, "Even if we are closed down for bad weather, you are going to get paid."

It didn't take too many days to figure out what the promotion really meant. If we were extra-busy I had to work eighty hours a week for the same amount of money. I realized he was guaranteeing there would be a cap on how much I could earn—that I could not make one dollar more than my salary, regardless of what happened.

I was locked into a fixed lifestyle because of time and money—and this dictated what I could do and what I could purchase.

Take the Lid Off

If you are told you have job security and you belong to a union, God bless you. Why do I say this? Because if the union decides to strike and you don't go back to work for two years, you'll run out of benefits. As so many have found out, the money doesn't last forever.

The only guaranteed income I know of is when you are captain of your own ship, working in an enterprise for yourself, in a proven pattern that can be replicated over and over again. You can set up as many businesses as you want with little expense—and reap a small percentage from each one.

Your security is in the ability to lay the foundation. This can be done by anyone at any age, but I especially encourage young people to launch their independent careers while they are strong and full of energy. The day may arrive when you lose your ability to perform at 100 percent capacity. But by then you have duplicated yourself with other independent business owners who have their own dreams, goals, commitment levels, and *whys*.

At this point, your operation will continue to run. As I have found it, income can become a steady, increasing stream.

This principle applies to many business models. There are thousands who own companies where their work can be replicated and rewarded through employees—and everybody wins. Some can produce income through trademarks, patents, and copyrights. Others may build independent sales teams who market an idea that is created or licensed.

Little becomes much when multiplication is involved. As the wealthy industrialist Andrew Carnegie once said, "I would rather have 1 percent of one hundred people's efforts than 100 percent of my own."

When you lift the lid off of your income, you can have anything you want.

Finally, a Choice

In my old job, I used to work six days a week and have one day off. Do you know how I found out when my day off would be? About forty-eight hours ahead of time—when they would post a schedule.

I couldn't have free time when I wanted to. It was not mine to decide. And on very cold or rainy days when we were forced to close, my boss would tell me, "Count those as your days off."

Regardless of what I planned, I was at the mercy of the

man in charge. When you have no dream, you have no choice.

Thank God, the moment finally came when I could stay at home and be a full-time husband to my wife. Yes, I was working hard at my new venture, but the hours were mine and I could choose when I got up, where I went, and how much time I wanted to spend with the family. Thankfully, our kids have never known a day when I had to work for another human being.

What's Your Aim?

Sadly, far too many settle for second best—or even third. And that's what they get in return.

I heard the story of a college professor who prepared a special test for his class of graduating seniors. He divided the test questions into three categories, instructing the students, "Choose questions from only one of the categories. The first category is the hardest and worth fifty points. The second is easier and worth forty points. And the third is the simplest, worth thirty points."

After the test, the students who had chosen the hardest questions were given an A—regardless of their answers. Those who had selected the middle category were given a B. And those who chose the easiest received a C.

As you can imagine, the students were frustrated with the grading of their papers and asked the professor what he was looking for. The teacher leaned over his lectern and explained, "I wasn't testing your book knowledge—I was testing your aim!"

Suits and Ties

When our boys, Ricky and Stephen, were six and eight years old, we were driving one morning in the Raleigh rush-hour traffic. The cars were bumper to bumper, moving at a snail's pace. Suddenly, Ricky, my inquisitive one, piped up and asked, "Daddy, why are all those people wearing suits and ties?"

I answered, "They are going to work."

Not satisfied, he asked again, "But why?"

I realized my answer was a little blunt when I told him, "Because they are crazy!" Then I clarified my words. "Well, they may not be crazy, but no one has ever showed them a way to escape their jobs."

"Isn't that what you do?" Ricky asked.

"Yes," I answered.

"Well, Dad, you need to show them all what you are doing."

I smiled and replied, "I'm working on it, son. I'm working on it!"

Please understand: every person makes choices regarding the road he or she will travel. For some, it means deciding on a career path that involves working for a corporation, a government agency, a hospital, or perhaps a school. These can all be noble professions. However, I believe everyone needs to look closely at their options and make sure that what they are doing will eventually lead to personal and financial freedom.

To this day, when Stephen and Ricky see someone wearing a suit and tie during the day, they shake their heads as if to say, *How crazy can they be?* Of course, my sons know these aren't unintelligent people, but people who just haven't found the freedom our family enjoys.

If your *why* is to be a full-time parent to your children, thank God for the motivation He is giving you.

Trapped in a Cage

When we were first married, Pam and I had no earthly idea what we could dream for and accomplish with our lives. We had mind-numbing jobs and were stuck in a routine that was leading nowhere.

You have to understand my perspective today. I have come to the place where I do not believe a person can truly become what God intends for him to be if he spends his life in a workaday environment. When your performance is based on what someone else requires or demands, you are not free to develop the skills and talents the Lord has placed within you.

It's like putting a powerful animal in a cage. If you confine a lion, tiger, or grizzly bear in a six-by-ten-foot cage, they can only stand up or lie down. It's impossible for them to use their awesome strength.

I believe there are millions of men and women who spend their entire adult life caged in careers that are not of their own choosing. As a result few use their true abilities because they aren't allowed to.

Don't Settle for Less

You cannot be a self-employed entrepreneur and have a business of your own with job mentality. It will absolutely destroy your chances of any success whatsoever. It's imperative that you rid your mind of the thinking, *I am going to do*

*a certain amount of work for a certain amount of time, and
I will receive a preapproved reward.*

You may rationalize, *Even though it's not everything
I would like, I'll get by. I can make it.* If you are thinking
that way when you are young, okay—as long as you have a
greater ambition. However, if you find yourself on the same
merry-go-round and still saying "I'll settle for that" when
you are 48, 58, or 68, the music is one day going to come to
a screeching halt.

How tragic to look back and realize you've had a life of
"settling."

Message on a Mirror

For a treat, I took my two boys to California for a father-
and-son weekend. There was a huge motocross event, and
we had scheduled some cross-training and coaching from
a seven-time national champion in the sport. Stephen and
Ricky were over the top with excitement. Unfortunately, the
weather didn't cooperate and the practice session was can-
celled, but we had time for some personal training.

The coach told my sons, "You guys know how to run and
do sit-ups, but I want to show you how to build some core
strength."

He explained that every muscle in the body is centered
around the stomach, and if your middle is strong the rest of
your body can really become powerful. He was teaching
Brazilian-American jujitsu techniques.

This fellow trained with Ultimate Cage Fighting champions—those crazy guys who get inside a wire cage and
don't come out until one is totally defeated.

In the training room there were no weights or workout machines—just mats on the floor and mirrors on the walls.

The coach told us, "We don't wear the white top and white pants with the belt. In fact, we don't award white, brown, or black belts. If that's your bag, fine. But we're not about flash—we are about results."

What I will always remember about that room were the big black letters posted on the mirror with these three words: EARN YOUR RESPECT.

This really hit home because in a business of your own, you can't demand respect. Just because you have a title on your lapel or a plaque on your wall doesn't mean you are a real leader. Leadership can be gained—and it can be lost. It's not a constant. Rather, it is based on the decisions you make, the effort you exert, the results you achieve, and how you treat others.

A Word to the Wise

One of the major reasons I chose this path was to make Pam proud of her husband. I wanted my wife to see me as giving my best, consistently and persistently, to not only provide for her now but to build a solid future.

Allow me to give a few words of advice to wives who may be reading this. If your husband is willing to spend his valuable time sharing his business opportunity, be thankful that you married a dreamer and a doer—because not every woman is so fortunate.

The good news today is that husbands and wives can be equal partners in all phases of success. I have also met wives who take the lead in building an independent enterprise while the husband continues his career path. Plus, thousands of singles are launching amazing business organizations.

Who Is Your Hero?

When Tara was about seven years old, after our business had started to take off, Pam took her to the movie *Robin Hood*. She was thrilled to see a hero who helped other people— even though his tactics may have been a little questionable. On the way home, Tara turned to her mom and asked, "Are there still heroes in the world like Robin Hood anymore?"

Pam looked at our daughter and replied, "Sure there are." Then, after naming a few individuals who had led heroic lives, she added, "But the biggest hero of all is your daddy. There have been many obstacles that have come into our lives, but he has overcome them all." She was speaking of the dragons of poverty, mediocrity, and fear. "I'm so proud of what he has done and what he has become."

Pam also used the moment as a teaching lesson. "Tara," she said encouragingly, "I want you to know that God has given you the ability to slay every dragon in your life, too."

I was filled with emotion when Pam shared this with me.

Two Voices

When you make a decision to break out of the mold, you start respecting *you*. In fact, the most important person I ever brought into my business was *me*. As long as I didn't quit I was going to make it.

One night, after two and a half years of effort, I drove

three hours to Charlotte, North Carolina, to make a presentation—and the person didn't even show up.

On the trek home, the negative guy on my left shoulder whispered, *What are you doing? Why are you spinning your wheels with so little to show for it?*

But the positive guy on my right shoulder countered, *You've been persistent and consistent for all this time. That's why you need to keep on keeping on—you are that much closer to success.*

Then Mr. Positive added, *Since you have found out you are capable of doing this when it isn't working, think how easy it will be when it is working. You've done the hardest part. Stay in just a little longer and start reaping the harvest of the seeds you have been planting.*

I'm so thankful I listened to that voice!

Pursue Your Purpose

Have you taken the time to answer the question "What is my *why?*"

Let me encourage you to not only think about this but to write it down on paper so you can read it again and again. Let the words become permanently etched in your thoughts and written on your heart.

This is the only way the reasons for your actions will make sense. Plus, life will take on new meaning when you pursue your purpose day after day.

You might start with a series of questions related to your current circumstances:

- Why should I build a business of my own?
- Why do I want to be financially free?

- Why do I want to spend more time with my family?
- Why do I want to financially support my church and worthy causes?
- Why do I want to help others succeed?

Take a close look at where you are at this particular moment in life, then ask yourself, *Where do I want to be one year from today? Or five years, or ten?*

To find your *why*, let me suggest that you take a look at your experiences. What gets you excited? What inspires and motivates you? What are your deepest values? What are the powerful, driving forces in your life you can identify?

This should not be something that is fuzzy or tucked away in the back of your mind. Your purpose is so important that it simply can't be left to chance.

More Than *What* and *How*

Far too many people launch into a new enterprise or start a program concentrating only on policies and procedures. They will make a list of what they need to do and how to accomplish it. You will most likely find step-by-step guidelines for various presentations, how the services or goods are to be delivered, and a detailed organizational chart.

This is the wrong approach. Before you ever take the time for the *what* and *how*, make sure you have clearly spelled out the *why*. Only then will there be meaning to your operation.

As a leader, you may know exactly why you are pursuing the goals you have established, but is this also clear to every member of your team? Don't assume everyone is on the same page. As often as possible, articulate the vision, go over the mission statement, and share your dream.

Remember, you want every aspect of your operation to be duplicable—and the best way for that to happen is for your associates to always make the same kinds of decisions you would make. Unless you continually share your *why*, how will they know what to do when you're not around?

A Powerful Connection

I sincerely believe if your reason for being is transparent, people who are introduced to your business or service will sense this almost immediately. Something inside them will click, and they will conclude, *I can trust these people. They know where they are going.*

As a result, you will be surrounding yourself with life-long, loyal friends who will stick with you in good times and bad. It's your *why* that forges a powerful connection between you and those you serve.

If, for any reason, your operation starts to veer off course, you need only to revert to your original vision statement to get back on track. Without a *why*, your best intentions could be derailed and defeated.

The results of a stated purpose will become evident in every aspect of your enterprise. You'll start to see high levels of innovation and creativity. There will be enthusiasm among team members, and you will be able to sustain your success.

However, think of what could happen without such a vision. If the decisions you make are unclear, no one is inspired to reach objectives. Actions will seem forced, even

phony. Even more, if the *why* isn't obvious, the how-to manual will have no focus or objective. This lack of direction
will soon spoil your business like rotten apples.

It is vital that you relentlessly pursue your reason for
being. As a result, you will have the right response to the
situations you face. There will be direction behind every
choice you make.

The Turning Point

Finding a purpose is what transformed the life of Moses,
who was an unassuming Jewish shepherd caring for his
flock on the back side of the desert. The turning point was
when he heard the voice of God speaking through a burning bush. It was so transforming that he eventually had the
courage to stand before Pharaoh, the king of Egypt, and
declare with authority, "Let my people go!"

In the words of Napoleon Hill, "There is one quality
which one must possess to win. And that is definiteness of
purpose, the knowledge of what one wants, and a burning
desire to possess it."

Changing Lives

It is my prayer that you wake up every morning with something more significant to do than pay a mortgage. If this is
your only driving force, you will eventually become a hollow shell of a person. I am convinced you can reach the
point where your *why* is about transforming lives.

I think about a couple whose marriage was on the rocks
twenty-five years ago. He was a hard-core biker, and she was

a chemist at a major pharmaceutical company. Alcohol was destroying their lives. After joining the team, they had to learn how to communicate with each other and work together. Suddenly, they had a dream and a future. Their marriage was restored, and they have two wonderful children. Today, we are the best of friends.

Filling the Vacuum

I have observed what has taken place in the turnaround of literally thousands of people and have come to this conclusion: when a man or woman has a new vision, the greatest problems can disappear.

Friend, when you grab on to a dream and it becomes a driving force, your negative distractions will diminish and become a thing of the past. I've seen this happen over and over again. Your new passion will completely envelop you and push the negative habit right out the door.

The abuse of drugs and alcohol can be related to people feeling bored, lonely and depressed, struggling with a poor self-image, and living a life without hope. When you fail to see yourself as a success, there is an empty hole, a vacuum inside that you will try to satisfy with all types of behaviors that are destructive and unproductive.

However, some may read these words and defiantly say, "I don't want to change. I like me the way I am."

How foolish.

That sounds like me before I turned in a new direction. I didn't know I was a loser, and there was nothing inside me that wanted to change or adjust. I was rocking along, polishing bumpers, emptying ashtrays, and applying tire gloss! I wasn't supermiserable—I was just numb.

Then I met a man with a spark in his eye, a bounce in his step, and an optimism about life that never diminished. Quicker than the snap of a finger, I realized, *That's what I want.*

Without really knowing it, I had been living like a zombie, looking for all the short-term pleasures I could find. But the day finally dawned when I no longer had a desire for partying—and I was ready to make a dramatic change.

A Cause and a Purpose

I've met those who decide to build a business of their own because they are night owls and want to sleep till the crack of noon! How cool is that?

It's not wrong to dream about buying a vacation house or a luxury car, but such material goals can become self-centered. There's so much more to living.

For me, my early motivation grew and changed until it became a cause and a purpose. Finally, when I had reached certain levels of achievement where my debts were paid and I was financially secure, instead of turning inward, I starting looking outward. My *why* became *How can I help others? What lives can I influence? How can I fulfill my God-designed destiny on this earth?*

As a result, my business has become a labor of love and a reason to wake up every morning. It is so much more fulfilling than chasing a dollar bill.

I pray you will stop making excuses and become driven by what truly matters.

8

You Were Created to Win

What God does, He does well.

—Jean de La Fontaine

Some people go through life and win what is called the Christopher Columbus Award. This is given to those who don't know where they're going, have no idea where they are when they arrive, and after returning home haven't a clue where they have been!

This is one award no one should strive for!

The dramatic turnaround I described in chapter 3 caused me to realize that every person is placed on this earth for a reason. I discovered that we were all created for greatness, with a purpose, and engineered to win.

I now know that every life is ordained and orchestrated by a higher power. It didn't happen by chance, but with forethought and purpose. This is why you need to start celebrating the fact that you are one of a kind.

Even before you drew your first breath, there was a plan

for you. I was touched by what was spoken by my Creator, "Before I formed you in the womb, I knew you. Before you were born I set you apart." And I read, "Even the very hairs of your head are all numbered."

Without question, you have a destiny that was designated before your birth. This may come as a surprise to many. I am constantly reminded of my purpose by the psalmist David, who wrote, "For you created my inmost being; you knit me together in my mother's womb. I praise you because I am fearfully and wonderfully made...Your eyes saw my unformed body; all the days ordained for me were written in your book."

God doesn't make mistakes or design junk, yet some choose to live as if He does. We were not planned to fail, even though many do just that. It's time to start living with the knowledge that you are a winner—the head and not the tail, a lender and not a borrower, a victor and not a victim.

What's Your Excuse?

I am reminded about a youngster in Ohio who was returning home from his first day at school. The teacher had told the class, "Tomorrow, I want each of you to bring a copy of your birth certificate so our school can be sure we have the right records."

However, *certificate* was a rather large word for the boy to remember—even though he had a general idea. When he arrived home, he bounced into the kitchen with his important message on the tip of his tongue: "Mom," he said, "tomorrow I have to take my excuse for being born."

The way he said it—an excuse for living—should make us all think. What is your excuse? What is your reason for being?

Limitless Thinking

Since I believe my Maker wants the absolute best for me, finding an opportunity that will bring success is part of this plan.

If you were a professional architect and designed the blueprint for your dream house, you would select the finest materials and pay attention to the smallest details. You would make sure every piece of wood was cut with precision and the highest-quality furnishings would adorn the interior.

I am encouraged to know that I am created in the same way—with a plan and a purpose. Nothing was left to happenstance. However, it is your obligation to make the choices and decisions necessary to move into your destiny.

Ralph Waldo Emerson once observed that the mighty power of the Gulf Stream will flow though an ordinary drinking straw—if the straw is placed parallel to the flow of the stream.

It's exactly the same with our own lives. If we align ourselves and allow a higher purpose to surge through our being, amazing achievements can happen.

I have learned to take my creative abilities and develop limitless thinking. Why? Because I serve a limitless God. I am a child of a King, not a pauper. I was formed in the exact likeness of my heavenly Father, and since He is a God of abundance, He has more than He needs and can pass blessing and favor down to His children.

Sadly, billions of people on this earth scrape by, living far beneath their potential.

There comes a time when you have to get alone and ask yourself some serious questions:

- What do I truly believe in?
- What are my guiding principles?
- What governs my actions?
- What do I stand for?
- What gives real meaning to my life?
- What qualities are essential for me to be complete?

The great English thinker C. S. Lewis said, "You never know how much you really believe in anything until its truth or falsehood becomes a matter of life and death. It's easy to say you believe in a rope to be strong as long as you are merely using it to cord a box. But suppose you had to hang by that rope over a precipice. Wouldn't you then first discover how much you really trusted it?"

Fulfill Your Purpose

Mark Twain told the story of a man who died and met Saint Peter at the pearly gates. Realizing Saint Peter was a wise and knowledgeable person, he decided to ask a question. "Saint Peter," he began, "I have been interested in military history for many years. Tell me, who was the greatest general of all time?"

Saint Peter quickly replied, "Oh, that's easy to answer. It is that man right over there"—and he pointed to a gentleman nearby.

The new arrival in heaven was taken aback, and responded, "You must be mistaken, Saint Peter. I knew that man on earth, and he was just a common laborer."

"That's right, my friend," replied Saint Peter. "But he would have been the greatest general of all time...if he had been a general."

You and I have been gifted with unlimited potential. As someone so aptly stated, "We have the equal ability to be unequal."

What will you do to fulfill your purpose? What steps will you take to accomplish your purpose here? My heart goes out to the man or woman who is not attached to a power beyond their own. Such a person is missing true peace, security, hope, and the very essence of life.

A Brilliant Discovery

Each of us is blessed with extraordinary creativity to use our minds to put concepts and ideas together.

As you have read, I spent years working at a car wash, but I never envisioned what a man named George Ballas saw one day as he drove his car through a wash tunnel.

As Ballas watched the nylon strings of the brushes surround his car, his mind relaxed and he began to think about the chores he had to do before the sun went down. High on his list was the tedious task of trimming and edging his lawn.

Like a bolt out of the blue, an idea struck him. He studied the brushes in the car wash again and watched them straighten out while revolving at high speed—yet remain flexible enough to reach into every nook and cranny.

He asked himself, *Why not use a nylon cord whirling at high speed to trim the grass and weeds around trees and the house?* Just like that—the Weed Eater was invented.

The first Weed Eater Ballas put together was rough and certainly needed some fine tuning. He punched holes in a popcorn can and threaded them with cord. Then he took the blade of his edger and bolted the can in place. His crude invention tore up the turf and made a terrible noise, but it whipped off the weeds just as he dreamed it would.

He decided to go commercial, but the first twenty distributors he approached thought his idea was crazy. "Cut grass with a nylon string? No way!"

Undeterred and not willing to take no for an answer, Ballas invested his own money in the first Weed Eater. It weighed thirty pounds. To introduce it to the public, he and his son filmed their own commercial, and he bought $12,000 worth of local television airtime.

Immediately, he was swamped with orders—and not just from the local area. Calls poured in from around the country. People were phoning their friends, and through word of mouth Weed Eater soon became a major international company.

Wow! As I can personally attest, amazing things can come out of a car wash!

This same kind of God-given creativity has resulted in thousands of breakthroughs. For example, a fellow named George de Mestral was brushing burrs out of his wool pants and his dog's fur when he became curious about the tenacity of the burrs. When he looked at them under a microscope, he saw hundreds of tiny hooks snagged in the mats of wool and fur. Later he made a mental connection, and Velcro fasteners were born.

The brain we are born with has unlimited potential.

A simple bar of iron might be worth ten dollars, but if you forged it into a horseshoe, it could be worth thirty dollars. And if you used it for making sewing needles, it could be worth much more. But if that same metal was refined and turned into watch springs, its value could increase to a quarter of a million dollars. The difference is in how we apply our creativity.

The question we need to ask is this: should we spend our time working on small ideas that yield small results or great ideas that produce dynamic and exciting results?

In his book *The Law of Success*, Napoleon Hill observes, "Just as the oak tree develops from the germ that lies in the acorn, and the bird develops from the germ that lies asleep in the egg, so will your material achievements grow out of the *organized* plans that you create in your *imagination*. First comes the thought; then organization of that thought into ideas and plans; then transformation of those plans into reality. The beginning, as you will observe, is in your *imagination*." [Italics in the original.]

Our ability to visualize, imagine, and create is a gift from above we need to cherish and value highly.

Your Compass

One of the most important discoveries on my journey was to realize that the Bible is my ultimate handbook for success. On its pages, the same Maker who spoke this whole ball of wax into being has a special Word.

It will be a compass that steers in the right direction and sets the boundaries between what is right and what is wrong. Embracing these eternal principles leads to results that are more than amazing.

I never look at the Bible as a book with chapters and verses; rather, it is a love letter written to me that is filled with promises. I take everything written as personal—and it inspires and guides my steps. Never, never has it led me in the wrong direction.

Some may read a particular passage and question, "Well,

that's not what it really means." But I have decided to stand firmly on every promise. What do I have to lose?

As I began filling my mind and heart with positive principles, I started listening to messages on speaking words of faith and hope. For example, King Solomon said, "Death and life are in the power of the tongue."

I learned that my thoughts control what I say, what I say controls my actions, and my actions control my destiny.

At first, my business certainly wasn't skyrocketing, but my self-image and confidence sure were. I couldn't track my progress on a computer spreadsheet, yet I was able to track it within myself. I *knew* I'd be a success if I just stayed the course and worked harder and smarter every hour or every day.

My Source of Supply

I was being set free from a world where I was not operating by any divine law. In fact, I was breaking many of them. On the outside I may have appeared strong and in control, but on the inside I had no power, no strength, no core values. I didn't know what I believed.

Here is one vital fact I discovered: I found that the car wash was not my true source of supply. I was excited when I read, "God shall supply all your need according to His riches in glory."

At that point, my success was not in the seen but in the unseen. As time went by, I began to visualize thousands and thousands of men and women deciding to follow their dreams. In the process they started to live by eternal truths, they cleaned up their act, and they were blessed beyond measure.

That vision became a reality.

An amazing thing took place. God's laws brought business principles to life, and those business principles allowed me to prove God's laws.

One of my passions was to achieve such success that people would say, "It can't be his education. It can't be his background, his personality, athletic ability, or work ethic. What can it possibly be?"

I want any observer to conclude that my success is only because of my relationship with my heavenly Father through His Son—and the result of applying the indisputable laws I have learned.

Nourishing the Seed

When I woke up to the fact that a higher power had given me the opportunity to succeed and nothing I did was by accident, I started putting two and two together.

Since I had the seeds of greatness inside me and was excited about the opportunity, I realized that, just maybe, this was what I was destined to do with my life. However, it was up to me to water, nourish, and develop that seed.

Instead of taking and keeping, I discovered the law of sowing and reaping. Like gravity, this law works. Believe me, the more you give, the more you receive. I have proven it again and again. A seed may be small, but it multiplies and brings in an awesome harvest—"exceedingly abundantly, above all that we ask or think."

Most men and women go through their entire life and never think—they just do. Like sheep, they blindly follow the crowd and take the path of least resistance.

This is not the blueprint designed for anyone—and it

doesn't begin to reflect what you are capable of. The seed of greatness lies inside every human being, yet some never do what is required to reap a bountiful harvest.

Simple Truths

I didn't suddenly become free when I began receiving large checks from my marketing company. My freedom arrived when I found out that I was put on this earth with a plan and a purpose—and it certainly wasn't to fail. I was liberated when I accepted God's offer to give me a clean heart and a renewed mind. Wow! What a defining moment that was for me.

Before that time I was broke mentally, spiritually, emotionally, and financially. Let's face it; I was damaged goods. But I am happy to report that I wasn't created that way. My condition was the result of who I associated with, who I listened to, what I watched and talked about. I was nothing more than a reflection of the social environment in which I was raised.

Today, I don't claim to have all the answers for the problems you face, but there is no confusion in my mind regarding how I am to live. The simple truths and fundamental principles I have learned sustain me. I also firmly believe that seeds of greatness were embedded in my heart, mind, and soul—and how they grow and multiply is my gift back to my Maker.

Two Copper Coins

In the Bible there is a story about Jesus watching as people put their money into the temple treasury. There were many wealthy men who threw in large donations, but then a poor widow came along and put in two small copper coins, worth only a few cents.

Jesus called His disciples together and told them, "Truly I tell you, this poor widow has put more into the treasury than all the others. They all gave out of their wealth; but she, out of her poverty, put in everything—all she had to live on."

Proportionally, she gave a million dollars. From this you and I can learn that money doesn't change you—it reveals you.

Keeping the Bargain

When we were growing our business, we came to the point where we fully understood why we had chosen this particular path. There was a much bigger picture involved than moving products or adding team members. One night Pam and I sat on the side of our bed and prayed, "Lord, if You raise us up and use us, we will never deny You. We will always give You the honor and glory for our success."

Without question, He met His part of the bargain, and we are keeping ours.

I trusted and believed that the promises I read would work for me, because He is "no respecter of persons." The Creator will always do what He says.

Nothing is going to grab you by the neck, and force you to act in a certain way. You are given the most amazing power imaginable—the power to choose.

The options you have are clear, but only you can make the decision regarding which ones to choose. No one is forcing you; it's up to you.

Etched in your DNA are not only special talents and abilities, but an assignment to be carried out. The decision to make it happen is up to you.

A Will for You

I don't believe you are reading this by accident. There is a plan for your life. You may ask, "What is it? I'd really like to know."

Let me share one of the most powerful verses I have ever read: "Beloved, I pray that you may prosper in all things and be in health, just as your soul prospers."

Please pay close attention to the words "in *all* things." Regardless of the challenges you experience, the greatest desire is that you prosper in all areas of your life: materially, physically, and spiritually.

This isn't referring to "pie in the sky in the great by and by" where everyone is supposed to be healthy, happy, and perfect. After all, nobody will be sick in heaven. So live in abundance *now*—on this earth—and you will prosper.

Winning is the objective, but your success is going to be in direct proportion to how much you are willing to change and grow. Once again, they didn't teach me this in high school!

Today, there is a vertical alignment in my life. God comes first, my family second, and my business is down the line. I make all of my decisions based on how it will affect any of these three priorities. If there is a potential harm to any one of the three, I back off.

Where Is Your Armor?

In our world today, there is a fierce battle being fought for hearts and minds. To put it in simple terms, good stands on one side and evil on the other.

Never forget that evil has only one objective: "to steal, kill, and destroy." Evil lurks around like a roaring lion, seeking whom he may devour.

Always with a conniving plan, evil seeks to find your weaknesses. If you attempt to make it through life by trying to avoid evil, you're in trouble because you have no armor, no shield, and no protection. You are defenseless on the front lines, fighting a battle without the right equipment. It's a recipe for failure.

This is why you should put on the shield of faith, the helmet of salvation, the breastplate of righteousness, and the sword of the Spirit. As I told a friend, "The only part of you the armor doesn't protect is your rear end—because you are not supposed to be sitting on it or retreating!"

Dressed in this armor, you can defeat evil and enjoy championship living.

"What If?"

As the acclaimed Irish playwright George Bernard Shaw was nearing the end of his life, a reporter challenged him to play the what-if game.

"Mr. Shaw," he said, "you have been around some of the most famous people in the world. You are on a first-name basis with royalty, world-renowned authors, artists, teachers, and dignitaries. If you had your life to live over and could be anybody you've ever known, who would you want to be?"

"I would choose," replied Shaw, "to be the man George Bernard Shaw could have been, but never was."

This was a stunning answer from a very successful person who knew he possessed much more potential that had remained untapped.

"No Excuse Sunday"

If you have drifted away from filling your heart, soul, and mind with what truly matters, perhaps it's time to make a new start.

I heard about a minister who announced to his congregation, "To make it possible for everyone to attend church next week, we are going to have a special 'No Excuse Sunday.'" Then he gave the details:

- "Cots will be placed in the foyer for those who say, 'Sunday is my only day to sleep in.'"
- "There will be a special section with lounge chairs for those who feel that our pews are too hard."
- "Eyedrops will be available for those with tired eyes— from watching TV too late on Saturday night."
- "We will have steel helmets for those who say, 'The roof would cave in if I ever went to church.'"
- "Blankets will be furnished for those who think the church is too cold and fans for those who say it is too hot."
- "Scorecards will be available for those who wish to list the hypocrites present."

- "Relatives and friends will be in attendance for those who like to go visiting on Sunday."
- "There will be TV dinners supplied for those who can't attend church and cook dinner, too."
- "We will distribute 'Stamp Out Stewardship' buttons for those who feel the church is always asking for money."
- "One section will be devoted to trees and grass for those who like to seek God in nature."
- "The sanctuary will be decorated with both Christmas poinsettias and Easter lilies for those who have never seen the church without them."
- "We will be providing hearing aids for those who can't hear the preacher and cotton for those who can."

I believe this list really covers it all!

Prosperous Principles

Over the years, I have heard many give their excuse for failure with the words, "Well, I'm only human."

Perhaps you'd better think twice before making such a statement! I am often reminded that I am not made in the image of man; rather, as I read in the first chapter of Genesis, I was created in my God's own image.

When you finally embrace this truth, it will raise your sights, lift your expectations, and let you know there is a marvelous plan for your future. If you only focus on your weaknesses, you'll wind up justifying and making excuses for your mistakes.

How are you going to live? By design, or by default?

There's No One Like You

Let me share the story of a famous musician who walked out on the stage before a concert and announced that he would be playing one of the world's most expensive violins. His first selection was played flawlessly, and there was a resounding applause.

The violinist graciously bowed, but then did the unthinkable. He took the violin and smashed it across his knee! The audience was stunned, and a silence fell across the concert hall.

"Don't worry," the smiling musician assured the crowd, "it's only a cheap counterfeit."

Next, he took out the expensive violin and began to play. However, most people could not tell the difference between the two instruments. Why? Because the quality of the instrument is secondary to the skill of the performer.

Here's the point. Whether you know it or not, you are a highly prized, unique instrument who has been custom-made. In fact, when you were created, God threw away the mold. There won't ever be another individual exactly like you.

Are you performing to the best of your potential? Are you measuring up to what your Maker intended for you?

The Person You Were Meant to Be

Ask yourself, *What is the purpose of my life?* Is it simply to make money, become well known, or just to have fun? Friend, these objectives will leave you empty—much like eating cotton candy at the state fair.

By now you surely know that my hope is for you to enjoy a prosperous, healthy, victorious existence here on earth. People will be drawn to you, not because of what you do but rather because of who you are.

When you are weary of walking the road of life alone, start living by eternal principles. Your world will never be the same.

I can't wait to hear your story.

9

FREE! TOTALLY FREE!

*Freedom means I have finally been set free to
be all that God wants me to be, to achieve all
that God wants me to achieve, and to enjoy all
that God wants me to enjoy.*

—Warren Wiersbe

Pam was eight months pregnant. She was still working at
the car wash cashier's window—and we didn't know if the
baby would be a boy or a girl.

I said to her, "In thirty days you're going to deliver our
first baby. Would you like to be a full-time mom and raise
your own children?"

"Desperately," she replied.

"You don't want to stay at the car wash, make a little
money, and put the baby in day care?"

"Absolutely not" was her answer. "I want to be the mother
of my kids." She couldn't imagine letting someone else
raise our children and perhaps teaching them bad habits or,

heaven forbid, running the risk of something going wrong. It wasn't worth trading for an extra $280 a week on the job.

After working our business for nearly five years, it was showing signs of life, so I rented a limousine for twenty-five dollars and decided to make a big deal out of her last day at work.

Actually, it was just a big car painted black. But we put two American flags on the front so if you squinted it did look like a limo—from a distance—when it was moving fast! A friend drove the car. He was dressed in a rented tux that was two sizes too small, and he looked like Barney Fife from *The Andy Griffith Show*.

I had balloons and flowers delivered, and about fifteen people in our business showed up for the send-off.

A month later, our precious daughter, Tara, came home from the hospital with a full-time mom. She has been blessed to be raised with a mother at home. Pam is still busy, traveling and speaking at major events in our business, but our children always come first.

The Big Change

As we progressed, we were able to return the beat-up Mustang back to Pam's parents. It drew its last breath and died with over three hundred thousand miles on the speedometer. With the money that was coming in we bought a used BMW.*

It wasn't long before I thought, *If Pam can be a full-time mom, why can't I be a full-time dad?*

In September 1989 I sold my lawn care business. It was as if a heavy weight had been lifted from my shoulders when I turned over my list of customers and deposited the check for the sale. No more estimates to give, no more equipment to repair, no more employees to organize. I was a free man—and have been ever since.

"It's Mine!"

The day our business began to flourish was when Pam decided to really get involved. I remember the Thanksgiving we were at her parents' home, and her mom asked, "Pam, how's your business going?"

She answered, "It's not mine; it's Larry's."

A couple of years later, when we began to have even more success, we were at a family function and her mother asked again, "How's Larry's business going?"

Pam was quick to reply, "It's not Larry's business; it's ours."

Later, when we became extremely successful, to the same question Pam answered, "It's not Larry's business; it's mine!"

Of course, she was just kidding. But she really enjoys cashing those checks!

The Missing Factor

My father was one of the greatest men in my life. He taught me many of the work habits I apply to what I am doing now.

However, there was one factor missing in his career plan. He didn't duplicate himself. His income was based only on his ability to perform at his gas station. Later he added a tow truck, a wrecker service, and a salvage business. It was a nice middle-class income.

When Dad took in a wrecked car, damaged beyond

repair, he'd strip out the wiring, take out the battery and radiator, and store the items in our garage.

Kids in the neighborhood would come over and tease, "Your dad must be a junk man. Look at all this stuff in your garage."

But my father knew exactly what he was doing. Once every two or three months, a truck would pull up and buy all the radiators. Another would come along and purchase the wiring or the batteries.

One day, Dad called me out to the garage. "Look, Larry," he said and showed me a wad of money clutched in his hand. "That guy just gave me $1,500 for those radiators."

This was his "fun money" to take us on a little vacation. He proudly told me, "You don't get this at a regular job."

He worked harder than the guy next door so he could have more than the guy next door.

It never bothered me what other people thought. My dad was a good father who did all he could do. Unfortunately, he ran out of hours in the week and days in the month. As hard as he worked he could not duplicate himself. So when he had to slow down, so did his income. Although he saved some money, his life outlived his savings.

Dad taught me this valuable lesson: don't worry about critics, because they aren't going to pay your bills.

A New Home

Earning my freedom may have seemed difficult at times, but not when compared to the alternative.

There were days in my landscaping service when I would climb a forty-foot ladder, reach my hand in a soggy gutter full of leaves, pull out the leaves, and dump them in a plastic bag. Then I'd climb back down, move the ladder a few feet, and repeat the process again and again—often working at six or eight houses a day. I was willing to do whatever it took because I had a dream.

During this period there was an expensive home being built on two and a half acres in Raleigh. It was a show house on display in the Parade of Homes, and it won many awards. At one time I had the contract to mow the lawn and clean the windows of that beautiful house.

Just a few years later, it was the home our family moved into when we became financially free. The only difference between me and my neighbors is that they drive to work every morning to pay the mortgage, while mine is totally paid for.* I have the privilege of spending the day having fun with my family and helping others.

This was a far cry from my work at the car wash, wiping dead bugs off chrome bumpers—or when we sold my childhood train set at a garage sale to buy milk and cereal for our babies.

Pam's Special Dream

I promised my wife that if she would help me grow my business, every one of her dreams would come true. Well, since she was a little girl, she would lie awake at nights, thinking of how wonderful it would be to own a horse.

In 1997, her childhood fantasy became a reality. That was when we purchased a thirty-four-acre horse farm with amazing stables. It used to be called Triangle Farms—considered the top horse-boarding facility in the Raleigh area.

Pam's first horse was named Cinnamon Bear, and as I write this her private herd now numbers thirteen horses.*

Life to the Fullest

Today, I am able to laugh at the struggles we faced. They were just a phase we had to pass through—and I would do them over again for what I know now.

Most of the rewards I cannot put a price on because they have to do with friendships and the people we have met along the way. Because of the benefits built into our business, we have been able to spend quality time with our friends on trips to Hawaii, the Caribbean, and many resorts in the United States.*

One of the many joys of freedom is waking up every day and doing whatever you please. It is helping a needy family without anyone knowing about it. Being able to afford a nanny to help with the children if you choose to. It is spending time with those who need encouragement. Simply, it is experiencing life to the fullest.

In a business that shows people how to be free, the "goodies" we often refer to grab the attention of those who are materialistic. Only later can we show them what truly matters—faith, family, friends, and freedom.

Success is not accumulating cars or houses; it is the person you become in the process.

None of the Drawbacks

Pam and I are average people who, because of the choices we have made, live an above-average life.

I was just an ordinary American who took a business opportunity, and I dedicated myself to its success—the hard part was not for my whole life, but for a few years. Many have done it in far less time.

I don't regret the commitment I made, because the bigger my business became, the more control I had over how I worked.*

I recently told a friend, "I get paid like a pro athlete or a celebrity, with none of the drawbacks."

I was thirty years old before I flew on an airplane for the first time. It wasn't the biggest plane in the world—and I think there were a few small farm animals on board with us! It didn't take long, however, until we were flying first class—and, even better, in a private aircraft. No early arrival for us, no long lines or security checkpoints. Just show up and go!

A free lifestyle means time and money—not just one of these, but both. Time with no money is a problem, but money with no time is worse.

We have to realize that no amount of cash can purchase extra days, hours, or minutes. Time is an extremely precious commodity and is to be used wisely.

Harvey Mackay, author of *Swim with the Sharks Without Being Eaten Alive*, said it well: "Time is free, but it's priceless. You can't own it, but you can use it. You can't keep it, but you can spend it. Once you've lost it you can never get it back."

I never undervalue or take lightly the hours I can now spend with my family.

Recently, in our business, we earned a week's vacation to any destination in the United States for our entire family. We chose Jackson Hole, Wyoming. Not only did we have an all-expenses-paid trip to an awesome resort, we also got to fly there and back in a Gulfstream V.

Here we were, traveling in a private plane that retails for $59 million and can fly up to 6,700 nautical miles at speeds reaching 590 mph. The onboard snacks were far better than peanuts and pretzels—they served fresh strawberries and gourmet goodies. What an incredible trip!*

I'm not bragging, just describing the fruits of our labor.

Turning Pro

As you've no doubt gathered, motocross racing has been a large part of my life and our family's lives for many years. Stephen and Ricky have been racing amateur MX almost forty weekends a year since 2000. Without the freedom we have, I don't know how this would have been possible.

Stephen has now retired from amateur racing to start his own business and partner with Pam and me. Ricky continued on and turned professional in 2010.

We were blessed with the free time and finances to attend almost all their amateur races, and now we are able to watch Ricky race as a pro. This is a dream come true for me, as I raced amateur MX as a teen. I always wanted to be a professional rider. I must admit, however, that both our sons are much better than I was, and they have accomplished higher levels in the sport.

A Great Day in L.A.

Since I have a passion for baseball, one of the goals I set several years ago was to visit every major league baseball stadium in the country—all thirty of them. I'm well on my way.

Number 19, Dodger Stadium in Los Angeles, was a

standout. Even though the Dodgers beat the St. Louis Cardinals 12 to 4, the score wasn't important. I was privileged to spend forty-five minutes with Hall of Fame broadcaster Vin Scully in his announcer's booth. We talked baseball, politics, and life. It was surreal, since I had listened to him on radio and television my entire childhood.

Plus, I also met Tony La Russa and Joe Torre—two of the best managers of all time and future Hall of Fame members.

It's a memorable trip I will never forget.

For a Dog?

Another of our family pleasures is having the time and means to keep whatever pets we want around the house.

I remember when our dog, Mikko, tore his knee. He's a beautiful white lab that weighs 115 pounds, but he's about as sharp as a marble! The only thing he responds to is food.

Mikko was limping, so Tara took him to the vet. "Bad hip," she was told. When he didn't improve, she took him to another vet. "Bad hip. Might have to replace it."

Still not satisfied, she went to a third veterinarian for yet another opinion: "Your dog doesn't have a bad hip; he has two bum knees."

It was time for an MRI. Good news: the hip was fine. Bad news: both knees were shot. "He needs major reconstructive surgery."

When I received the bill, it was $5,000 per knee—for a *dog*!*

On arriving home, Mikko was still limping badly. "I don't think the surgery worked," I told Tara and Pam.

Next, I learned he had to go into rehab because he had developed tendinitis. So off went Mikko for six weeks of physical therapy—a place with a treadmill, a special harness, daily massages, and a personalized diet. Another $1,800—for a *dog*!*

All I was thinking as I wrote out the check was, *Thank God I am financially free!*

"I'm Proud of You"

My father passed away when he was eighty-seven. He had lived a good life and provided for his family the best he could. But the day came when the tables were reversed and it was my turn. I gladly helped him with whatever he needed. There were no regrets.

If I had listened to the advice of my mom and dad earlier, I wouldn't have started the particular business I chose. They warned me, "You're getting in too late. All the successful people have already done it before you"—and they gave me the reasons why it wouldn't work.

I had to make a personal decision. Would I listen to my parents or to those whose lifestyle I wanted to emulate?

The last time I ever talked to my dad, I held him in my arms. He was too weak to sit up. His body was a shadow of its former self, but his mind was still sharp. He told me, "Son, take care of your mom. I'm very, very proud of you."

In the final months, my dad could no longer care for my mother, and she needed round-the-clock help. I considered it a privilege to be able to spend $15,000 a month for three nurses.

I loved my parents and am so thankful I was able to honor them in this way.

Solving the Problem

Please understand: I don't hate your job—I just despised mine. If you love what you do, keep doing it, but here's the litmus test. Do you really enjoy setting the alarm clock every morning and going to work, or have you just learned to deal with it because you have no other options?

Of all the compartments of life we have to conquer—family, finances, health, etc.—most spend forty years or longer working on the money part, but at the end of the journey it's still not solved. Why? Because they have not built a vehicle that can produce a steady stream of income.

I love teaching people how to duplicate themselves and compound their time and effort.

Wealthy people don't get rich by clipping coupons or putting a few dollars aside for a rainy day. Instead they look at their financial needs and outearn whatever it takes to provide for a debt-free future.

Show the Way

One of the proven ways to expand your mind is to latch on to a bigger dream. When you're making $40,000 a year, it's hard to think about owning a condo in the Caribbean or driving a Porsche.

Eventually, your income will reflect what you see yourself capable of becoming. So when you broaden your dreams, your earnings and assets will also expand. But if you don't have a plan to achieve this, a ceiling will remain on your potential.

This is why I encourage you to change your thinking.

When you reach a certain point financially, you no longer scour the newspaper ads looking for bargains. You are not so concerned about saving six cents on a tube of toothpaste. Rather, you have the time and energy to put your creative mind into high gear—building even more businesses that can produce more income and show more people the path to financial freedom.

No matter how hard you work as an independent business owner, there is light at the end of the tunnel. You have one less worry. No longer will you be asking, "Can I afford it?"

The Thrill of Victory

There is nothing quite like putting in concentrated effort that will pay dividends for not only your life but for the lives of your children.

That was what I did to experience freedom. Freedom from alarm clocks and rigid schedules. In fact, with every year that goes by there are fewer days I wear a suit and tie.

Can you remember the exciting moments in your past?

Well, they don't have to end. Even though we have tasted so much of this banquet called life, every morning is still thrilling to wake up to, and another adventure is just around the corner.

I invite you to recapture that feeling of pitching a Little League baseball game or making the cheerleading squad. Remember the moment when you were a running back for your high school football team? You hit a hole in the line, and even though there were three guys chasing you, you crossed the goal line and scored the winning touchdown.

Most people can never relive those moments, but with a

business of your own, you can once again experience the thrill of victory.

As Americans we are blessed to live in the land of the free, and I will defend your decision to live an ordinary life. That is your choice. But please know that there are no limits on what you can achieve—even though there are some who would like to hold you back.

I will fight for anyone's right to be average, but I ask them to fight for my right to be successful.

A True Believer

With every passing year, Ronald Reagan's stock rises as one of the great presidents of the United States. But his critics didn't give him much of a chance when he decided to run for president. "After all," they exclaimed, "he's just a Holly-wood actor. How can he run the country?" Yet he put his stamp on our nation and made a tremendous difference in the world. He stemmed the tide of decay, and his beliefs benefited people of all persuasions, because they were true.

Today, there are many who run for office and say, "I am just like Ronald Reagan." Hardly. Most are not even close!

Reagan saw how helping people and keeping the country free go hand in hand. This sentiment seems to be forgotten in today's culture.

A Price to Be Paid

Unfortunately, the nation is divided between two mind-sets: (1) Does the government become my provider and take care of my family? Or (2) do I provide a good life for those I love?

I don't mind paying my fair share of taxes, but I become

concerned when I support an educational system that does not promote self-employment, free enterprise, or a wealth mentality.

These are issues worth defending.

As President Reagan once said, "Freedom is a fragile thing and is never more than one generation from extinction. It is not ours by inheritance; it must be fought for and defended constantly by each generation, for it comes only once to a people. Those who have known freedom and then lost it have never known it again."

Freedom isn't free, and financial independence is something you have to work for. Yes, there is a price to pay for success, but a much larger one to pay for failure.

The brave souls on the *Mayflower* didn't spend two months on a boat to come to America to work for IBM. They came for the opportunity to be free.

What was the cost of America's freedom? It can't be measured in dollars, but rather by the twenty-five thousand brave men who paid the ultimate price during the Revolutionary War. They knew that freedom was worth giving their lives for because it is so rare and precious.

Ask yourself: *What do I truly believe?* If you have only heard one side of the story of an opportunity, it's hard to embrace what may seem foreign and new. I pray the message of freedom will come through so loud and clear that you will welcome it with open arms.

The Pillar of Our Society

With every year that passes, I become more passionate about free enterprise. I believe it is the only system that gives dignity to the individual and causes society to flourish.

Daily, the media reports stories of poverty and the financial issues of our society. These reports stir debate among
everyone: from the affluent and the middle class to the
working poor and the impoverished. And while everyone
has an opinion as to who should fund public aid, who is
taking the initiative to provide opportunities for change?

As entrepreneurs we help provide opportunities, and
we create a hunger for success. In fact, this spirit that I call
free enterprise encourages people to better their skills and
develop their talents. The one bedrock principle of free
enterprise is that men and women are allowed to take risks
and build businesses of their own. Sure, I believe in com-
passion, but not when it becomes a substitute for personal
initiative. When that pillar is attacked, so is our way of life.

To me, free enterprise not only represents the best economic system, it encompasses much more:

- It gives men and women the liberty to make their own
  decisions.
- People can choose what they will do with their talents
  and abilities—with no limitations.
- It increases productivity, since the sky's the limit.
- Because it involves competition, we are able to purchase the widest variety of goods at the lowest possible prices.
- It promotes innovation, because if there is any kind
  of demand, free enterprise will create and supply the
  solution.
- It spurs high quality, since people have a choice between
  similar products and always want the best.
- It allows individuals to pursue their dreams and choose
  their livelihoods.
- It creates businesses that provide income for millions.

- It causes men and women to offer their best personal service.
- When business is left alone and driven by true market forces, everyone benefits.

I pray that free enterprise, the engine of our society, will withstand every force that comes against it and shine even brighter as an example for the world to follow.

True Freedom

Personally, I'd rather be broke and have a dream than be a multimillionaire without one. I am convinced that it is the dream that truly matters—the pursuit, the overcoming, the *be*-coming.

I will spend as much time as I can for the rest of my life encouraging people to start their own businesses. If not enough men and women accept the challenge, the day may arrive when we *all* lose our freedoms.

Today, the enterprise Pam and I poured our lives into produces millions of dollars every year.* I don't mention this to brag, but to let you know that if you put in the work, the results of your efforts can multiply beyond belief.

Now I can honestly say, "If I can do it, so can you." These aren't trivial words, they are the truth.

Are you ready to be free?

10

Now It's Your Turn!

The real man is one who always finds excuses
for others, but never excuses himself.
—Henry Ward Beecher

Excuses? There are a million of them floating around, but they are nothing but lies you keep fooling yourself with to escape doing what you know is right. Yet, if you continue to hold onto them, you'll remain in the status quo and life will pass you by.

Here's how some people justify their failure to act:

"I don't have enough time."

Many use this for avoiding exercise, widening their circle of friends, or launching a business. What they are really telling you is: *This isn't my priority.*

We all are given the same twenty-four hours in a day. If

you put a clock on your activities, I'm convinced you would be shocked at how many hours are being wasted.

Time, or the lack thereof, is not the issue—the problem is your desire to use it wisely. Start asking yourself, *How much time am I willing to set aside to gain my financial freedom?* You have more hours available than you think.

"I don't know how."

You might as well admit the truth and say, "I'm really lazy. I don't want to learn."

It's not necessary to take a college class to gain specific knowledge. The same facts are as close as punching the topic into Google on your computer.

As a child did you stay on a tricycle with the excuse, "I don't know how to ride a bike"? No, you persevered with your big two-wheeler until you got your balance and rode away.

It's the same when you decide to learn how to build any enterprise. One bit of information is added to another, and before long you're an expert on the topic.

"I don't have enough money."

Nonsense! If I could jump-start an independent business when my take-home pay was less than $400 a week after taxes, think what you can do. Using this excuse is telling yourself, *I don't want this bad enough.*

If the lack of funds is really the problem, put in a few extra hours, and you'll have the capital to get going. Let me remind you that some of the most profitable enterprises in the world were started on a shoestring.

Remember, the money it takes to build your business should never be seen as an expense; it is an investment in your dream. Your account can't increase until you plant the first seed.

"I don't have the right skills."

Very few individuals are born with a gift or talent that is so off the charts they never have to take a lesson or practice.

How do you know you can't play the guitar? Have you ever had a musician show you a few chords and then followed through on their instructions?

Skills aren't in your DNA; they are the result of actions repeated over and over until you master them. The average person can perform at a high level if they give themselves the chance to try.

Just as success is a planned event, so are the skills and talents you bring to the table.

"I'm not a good communicator."

What a cop-out! I can say this because of what I saw in my own wife, Pam. When I tell you she was scared to death to stand before a group of any size and speak, I'm not exaggerating. She would break out in a cold sweat and visibly start shaking.

However, when she realized she had something valuable to share, she forgot about her fear. I am so proud of her. Today she is one of the strongest speakers you will ever hear.

If I were to ask one of your close friends what it's like to have a conversation with you, hopefully they would respond, "No problem at all. I enjoy our talks together." Well, speaking to a stranger, or even to an audience, really isn't that different. Just share what is in your heart and the communication will flow effortlessly.

"My friends will laugh at me."

You have to make a choice. Are you so proud that what other people think outweighs the rewards that come from a thriving enterprise?

Millions are being held back because they dread to think how their so-called friends might respond if they tried something new.

Please don't let anyone pull your chain! In the long run, people will only laugh if you decide to abandon your dream and quit. I'm sure this is not on your agenda.

"I'm too young." Or, "I'm too old."

I've met entrepreneurs who started at the age of thirteen— and others who launched out in their seventies and eighties. Grandma Moses didn't even pick up a paintbrush until she was nearly eighty years old—and she created over fifteen hundred works of art before she turned one hundred!

Age is nothing more than a number. What you have to offer has no relationship to the date on your birth certificate.

"I don't come from the right background."

The side of the tracks you were raised on has absolutely nothing to do with success. In our organization we not only team with doctors, lawyers, and bankers, but those who are from any profession, education level, or upbringing. Those who were given no hope for a normal life have an opportunity for a successful one.

If you are unhappy with your circumstances, change

them. It's not your background that makes the difference, but your backbone!

You've Got to Be Kidding!

When presented with an opportunity, it's easy to flip it off and remark, "I couldn't do it because of...[this or that]."

I heard about a farmer who asked his neighbor if he could borrow a rope. "Sorry," the neighbor replied. "I am using it to tie up my milk."

"You can't use a rope to tie up milk," responded the confused farmer.

"I know," said the neighbor, "but when you don't want to do something, one excuse is as good as another."

A department of human services received this excuse from a man who refused to pay his required child support. He wrote, "I can't afford to pay. I'm too far behind on my cable bill."

Another delinquent, who was ordered to pay twenty-five dollars a week in alimony, complained, "I will not allow my ex-wife to get rich on my money!"

Then there was the woman who was placed on a strict diet, but cheated one morning by buying donuts at a Krispy Kreme shop. When asked why, she responded, "It's God's fault—for opening up a parking space right in front of the donut store as I was driving by!"

Take a close look at your excuses. Do they pass the test?

Be Thankful for the "Rough Spots"

Some people stay on the sidelines claiming they have too many "imperfections." That reason just doesn't fly.

If you ever visit a golf museum, you'll notice that the golf balls from the early days of the sport look much different from those used today. The first ones were very smooth.

As it is told, there was once an avid young golfer who didn't have enough money to buy a new ball, so he played with the only one he owned—and it was really beat up with plenty of dents and bruises. His playing partner was surprised that his brand-new golf ball didn't fly as straight or travel as far as his friend's.

That one observation led to what we have today: golf balls with literally hundreds of tiny dimples. These "rough spots" add to the ball's accuracy and distance.

It's the same with you and me. Our imperfections allow us to sharpen our performance.

Five Wasted Years

I once asked a fellow what he does with his spare time. "Oh, I just love to watch game shows like *Jeopardy!* or *Wheel of Fortune,*" he replied.

"Why?" I wanted to know.

He smiled. "I get a kick out of seeing the contestants win all that money."

"How long have you been hooked on those shows?" I asked him.

"About five years," he answered.

"Well, how much money have you made from watching?"

The question stumped him. "Not a dime," he finally had to admit.

Brilliant! Such a waste of precious time doesn't make a lick of sense to me. This guy could retire earlier if he invested the same amount of hours into a worthwhile personal enterprise!

You can get a handle on your situation by determining which factors you can control. Take charge of those first and then start on a course of action.

You may think, *But I can't harness time.* That may seem true, but you certainly can determine the priorities you assign to your schedule.

An Excuse a Month

A small-town store owner in Iowa was about to lose his business. It's no wonder when you look at the reasons he gave for his slow sales:

- January: People spent all their cash for the holidays.
- February: All the best customers have gone south.
- March: It's unseasonably cold and too rainy.
- April: Everybody is preoccupied with income taxes.
- May: There's too much rain, and farmers are distressed.
- June: There's too little rain, and farmers are distressed.
- July: The heat has everyone down.
- August: Everybody is away on vacation.
- September: Everybody is back from vacation, and they're broke.
- October: The customers are waiting to see how the fall clearance sales turn out.
- November: People are upset over the election results.
- December: The customers are saving money for the holidays.

What a wasted year!

Outrun Your Circumstances

You may feel the problems of life are gaining ground on you. Well, it doesn't have to be that way. Make a decision to step to the front.

A couple who were dating at a college in Vancouver, British Columbia, decided to go backpacking one weekend. They were up in the mountains when the young man spotted a grizzly bear stalking them. He panicked, but his girlfriend calmly took off her hiking boots and put on a pair of running shoes.

"What good will that do?" her boyfriend wanted to know. "You can't outrun a grizzly."

While she was lacing up her shoes, the woman responded, "I know. I just have to stay ahead of you!"

There's a lesson in this story. You can either let the challenges you face in your business sap your energy and set you off track, or you can decide to focus on solving them and get back on the road to success!

A House of Failure

If you are building a future that requires others to become involved, there is no shortage of people who are ready to latch on to an idea that feels right for them. And the opposite is also true: there is no shortage of wimps, whiners, and winos.

There are millions of men and women at this very moment who could shake the world if they found the right opportunity. But some use the weakest excuses for not even taking a look: "I had a flat tire," or, "I've got to visit my aunt."

Author Don Wilder is right on when he says, "Excuses are the nails to build a house of failure."

Since time is short, don't waste your hours on the tire kickers who are "just looking." If your business involves building a team of associates, get past the introduction, qualify their interest, let the "maybe"s leave, and spend your quality time with those who are ready to go for the gusto!

Alibis Are for Quitters

If you want to play basketball at a higher level, it makes sense to talk to someone who's at the top of their game. Only a fool would take advice from a player who dropped off the high school team after a couple of years with excuses: "They didn't give me enough playing time." Or, "The coach didn't like me."

It is no different in the business world. If you take advice from poor people, you will get poor advice. This is not an indictment against that person; it is an observation.

How many statues or memorials have you seen built to critics? This honor is reserved for overcomers. They are the individuals I listen to, and I absorb what they tell me—and I make my decisions accordingly.

Now that Pam and I have built a large, successful organization, there are many events where people like to shower us with accolades and applause. You can rest assured that our feet are firmly on the ground. We know where we came from, and we will never let it go to our heads.

The great church leader Charles Spurgeon counseled, "Every man needs a blind eye and a deaf ear, so when people applaud, you'll only hear half of it, and when people salute, you'll only see part of it. Believe only half of the praise and half of the critics."

One thing for sure. You have to forget about the naysayers and the dream stealers. They are a dime a dozen. I've heard it said that the moon couldn't go on shining if it paid any attention to the dogs who bark at it!

When I hear about judgmental people it reminds me of the two taxidermists who stopped before a window in which an owl was on display. They immediately began to criticize the way it was mounted. One commented, "The eyes are not natural, and its wings are not in proportion with its head."

The other man put in his two cents: "The feathers aren't neatly arranged, and the work on the feet could definitely be improved."

When they had finished their criticism, the old owl turned his head—and winked at them!

Something More

What a jolt to my senses when I discovered I was more than a busboy, more than a car wash manager, more than a salesman, and more than a landscaper.

At twenty-four I wasn't a bad person, just uninformed. I didn't know what really mattered or what was important— and frankly, I didn't care. After motocross racing, I'd sit with the guys around a campfire drinking beer because I thought, *This is what real men do.*

I didn't give a thought to the flag that flies over our nation. I had no knowledge of the meaning of Normandy or Omaha Beach, and I had no idea what took place at the Battle of the Bulge.

The term *free enterprise* wasn't in my vocabulary. I was absolutely clueless. I was a pawn being shuffled around the chessboard by the moves of other people. I was insignificant, wasting my life—looking for happiness on a softball field or at the bottom of a beer bottle.

A Breath of Fresh Air

While the car wash may have provided a meager roof over my head, it was also a leash around my neck. I could walk a certain distance, but I was yanked back just like a dog.

However, once I found out what was hidden inside me, there wasn't any excuse that was going to hold me back. I've never confessed to being the brightest bulb in the hallway, but when I first heard the opportunity I chose to hitch my wagon to, I knew, *This is going to be great.*

It was a breath of fresh air when I finally discovered who I was and where I was headed. Nothing was going to stop me except myself—and I wasn't about to let that happen. I was gaining tremendous confidence.

Without question, there were many crossroads—confusing intersections where I had to stop and figure things out. But when I successfully passed through a few of these, the travel became easier.

One of the thoughts I live by was first stated by Napoleon Hill: "In every adversity there lies a seed of equal or greater benefit."

I don't believe God gives you a struggle you can't handle or a dream you can't accomplish, because with His help all things are possible.

Core Values

In our organization, we have established eight core values that exemplify a character of excellence. They are the standards by which our affiliated business owners operate.

How many of these do you already possess, and which ones do you need to work on?

#1: Faith

We believe in having complete trust and a firm belief in something for which there is no proof.

#2: Service

We consider helpful acts and contributions to the welfare of others to be important.

#3: Unity

We find value in continuous purpose or action without deviation or change. This is the quality or state of unifying and the becoming of one.

#4: Honor

We find importance in a character's reputation, giving them a good name or public esteem. One's performance should be guaranteed by their given word and contain a firmness and moral excellence.

#5: Freedom

We acknowledge independence and liberation of slavery from the power of another as an important factor. We value the absence of necessity, coercion, or a constraint in choices or actions.

#6: Vision

We are great believers in the dream and achieving a strongly desired goal or purpose.

#7: Duty

We think highly of binding tasks, conduct, service, or functions that arise from one's position in either life or in a group. This becomes the force of a moral obligation.

#8: Courage

We encourage both the mental and moral strengths to venture, persevere, and withstand danger, fear, or difficulty at any level.

A Warning

As you can tell, I am pumped up about a person owning his or her own business. On these pages I may have come across rather tough on people who take a job for their career. Please understand, there is nothing wrong with a job if this is what you choose for your future. But when you are hammered by the economy and get replaced and fired in the coming years, please don't say you weren't warned.

I take pleasure in talking about personal financial freedom. What's the harm in looking at an opportunity where nobody is controlling you and you can enjoy ongoing income?

Pam and I built our business on faith, but we continue to expand it on belief because we have seen firsthand that it works.

Carving Out the Hours

How much time are you willing to put into what you are launching? At first you may be able to carve out only a few hours a week, but with success comes freedom—and you can invest more hours.

Then, when your belief level is raised because of the evidence you see, you'll reach the point where you ask yourself, *What* type *of hours will I invest?* You will have to balance your time among customers, associates, data entry, and the other details involved.

These are variable, but for financial security, you have to develop a taproot—the vision that carries the nutrition into your organization and gives it health and strength.

Get "Yourself" in Order

I still consider myself a work in progress.

Since we are all continuing the development of being better persons until the day we die, I pray from the bottom of my heart that you separate the original steps of building a business from the long-term process of getting *yourself* in order. Be careful not to confuse the two.

The earlier you develop your dream, the better. Once it takes root and begins to blossom, it can always be with you. You don't need to lose it when you get old, because the dream can stay alive.

As football coach Lou Holtz observed, "If what you did yesterday seems big to you, you haven't done anything today." Your dream must never die.

In a nutshell, life boils down to how much you want to take action on your vision. Remember, it's not talent or ability, it is decision and determination.

How frustrating to see men, women, and young people who are throwing away their tremendous potential.

Don't Quit Now!

Friend, you are much too close to the finish line to give up now. Don't even allow such a thought to cross your mind.

I often share the story of the high school basketball coach who was attempting to motivate and inspire his players to persevere through a difficult schedule. Halfway through the season, he stood before his team in the locker room and asked, "Did Michael Jordan ever quit?"

The team responded, "No."

Then he shouted, "What about the Wright brothers? Did they ever give up?"

"No," the team yelled back.

"Did Joe Montana ever quit?"

"No," they loudly responded in unison.

"Did Elmer McAllister ever quit?"

Suddenly, the room went quiet, and after a long silence

one player had the boldness to ask, "Who is Elmer McAllister? We never heard of him."

The coach snapped back, "Of course you never heard of him—he quit!"

New Possibilities

Leadership authority John Maxwell, a friend and mentor who has spoken to our organization at national conventions, believes, "When we become conditioned to perceived truth and closed to new possibilities, the following happens: We see what we expect to see, not what we can see. We hear what we expect to hear, not what we can hear. We think what we expect to think, not what we can think."

There are times I feel like a driving instructor. If I can teach a person how to shift from reverse to drive, it's been a fantastic day!

When you have a chance and a choice to succeed, things still matter, but at a higher level. Then, as you start sharing and passing the dream on to others, a miracle takes place. All of a sudden you are having an impact on the world. What a satisfying feeling that is.

In my own case, the larger my enterprise becomes, the more I am concerned with what is happening nationally and internationally—because I have so much more to lose.

A phrase I heard years ago stays with me: "All that is necessary for evil to triumph is for good men to do nothing."

If we are not awake and alert, those with wrong intentions can snatch our rights and freedoms away one at a time—while we are watching a football game or playing Scrabble. We won't even know what happened.

Go with Your Instincts

The insecure and nervous ask themselves, *What can I do? How can I make it?*

The only one who will determine where you will be twelve months or twelve years from now is you. Instead of trusting your intellect, go with your instincts, your common sense that lets you know, *I am capable of doing this.*

It is dangerous to wait for a crisis to erupt before you start asking the critical questions. Most people begin with, *How can I make this problem go away? What's the most convenient, easiest solution?*

Instead, you should be asking, *What is best for my family, my business, and my future in the long term?*

If you have that gnawing, churning feeling inside telling you to do something bigger and better than normal, what are you waiting for?

I like Benjamin Franklin's advice: "Well done is better than well said."

More Than a Decision

A third-grade teacher asked her class, "Suppose you had five birds sitting on a wire and three of them decided to fly away. How many birds would you have left on the wire?"

A little girl raised and wiggled her hand, confident of her answer. "There would be two birds left."

The teacher smiled and said, "No, there would still be five birds on the wire."

Then she explained that just because they *decided* to fly

away doesn't mean they actually did. You see, making a decision without acting upon it is a waste of thinking.

Will Rogers made this keen observation: "Even if you're on the right track, you'll get run over if you just sit there."

Stay Steady

Tonight, before you hop into bed, place a pen and a notepad on your nightstand. Then tomorrow, when you wake up, write these words in big letters: NO EXCUSES!

You are blessed to live in a land of freedom and free enterprise, where at the time and place of your choosing you can start and build a profitable business. You are not forced to live an average, mediocre life. You can be successful beyond imagination.

When you are working your plan, stay steady and focused, and don't allow others to shake your tree.

Take it from a higher authority. As the apostle Paul wrote long ago, "Let us not grow weary in well doing, for in due season we shall reap if we do not lose heart."

You will never know what you are made of until you step out in faith, turn yourself loose, and find out.

How would you like to never be stuck in rush hour traffic again? How would you like to throw away that annoying alarm clock? I hate that word *alarm*. It sounds like you have to put out a fire every morning!

Success is within the grasp of every human being. It is a choice you make.

No More Excuses!

What we've been discussing is not a dress rehearsal or a game; it is your life—and you only live it once. It's not like paintball, where if you fail to capture the flag the first time, you get another shot.

In life, there are no redos, but you can renew your efforts along the way to transform your dream into a reality, so make every precious minute count. The future is yours for the taking.

A skeptic may ask, "Do you really think you'll be successful?"

If you have made the right decision, you can look them square in the eyes and say with assurance, "I already am!"

This is true, because of the YOU-turn you've made on the inside.

NO MORE EXCUSES—live your dream!

A DECLARATION OF FREEDOM

More than 230 years ago, Samuel Adams, one of the Founding Fathers, closed his memorable speech to the Continental Congress with these words:

> If ye love wealth greater than liberty, the tranquility of servitude than the animating contest of freedom, go from us in peace. We ask not your counsels or arms. Crouch down and lick the hands which feed you. May your chains sit lightly upon you, and may posterity forget that ye were our countrymen.

About the Author

Larry Winters is an entrepreneur and motivational speaker. Through humor and passion, Larry shares his life experiences and business philosophy to empower others to pursue their dreams.

He is the founder and president of Leadership Team Development (LTD) Inc., a company that provides business support materials for Amway business owners in North America.

Larry was born in Camden, New Jersey, and lived there with his family until, at age sixteen, they moved to Raleigh, North Carolina.

Larry is passionate about motocross, baseball, photography, and traveling with his family. He currently resides in Raleigh with his wife, Pam. He lives near his three grown children: Tara and her husband, Matt; Stephen; and Ricky.

APPENDIX

Amway Income Disclosure Policy

Income disclosures listed below pertain to the AMWAY™ Business Opportunity and becoming an Amway Independent Business Owner (IBO).

> **The average monthly Gross Income for "active" IBOs in the US was $202.**

Approximately 46% of all IBOs of record were "active."

US IBOs were considered "active" in months in 2010 when they attempted to make a retail sale, or presented the Amway IBO Compensation Plan, or received bonus money, or attended an Amway or IBO meeting. If someone sustained that level of activity every month for a whole year, their annualized income would be $2,424. Of course, not every IBO chooses to be active every month. "Gross Income" means the amount received from retail sales, minus the cost of goods sold, plus monthly bonuses and cash incentives. It excludes all annual bonuses and cash incentives, and all non-cash awards, which may be significant. There may also be significant business expenses, mostly discretionary, that may be greater in relation to income in the first years of operation.

> **The average monthly Gross Income for "active" IBOs in Canada was $181.**

Approximately 66% of all IBOs of record were "active."

"Active" means a Canadian IBO attempted to make a retail sale, or presented the Independent Business Ownership plan, or received bonus money, or attended a company or IBO meeting in the year 2000. "Gross Income" means the amount received from retail sales, minus the cost of goods sold, plus the amount of Performance Bonus retained. There may also be significant business expenses, mostly discretionary, that may be greater in relation to income in the first years of operation.

The success depicted in this profile may reflect income from sources other than Amway, such as earnings from the sale of Business Support Materials or other businesses and investments.

Before registering as an Independent Business Owner (IBO) powered by Amway, you should read and understand the AMWAY™ Business Opportunity Brochure, which contains important information for those interested in becoming IBOs.